Welcome to Fresh-Beginning's cookery book "You Can Cook".

The driving force behind "You Can Cook" is Barbara Freeman, who brings together 20 years of experience in hotel and restaurant management, as well as private catering, with a love of good food and passion for creating delicious meals using simple tools and a deep understanding of ingredients. From cooking on a budget to crafting beautiful menus, our goal is to help you cook well and eat better, making mealtimes a positive experience for families and individuals.

Barbara has dedicated the past few years to conducting cooking sessions in local communities, where she recognised the need for a resource like this book to assist people in learning to cook. The aim of the cooking sessions is to empower individuals with the skills needed to prepare homemade meals for themselves and their families. The book is designed to inspire and motivate families and individuals to learn to cook, especially those who are struggling on a budget.

Barbara Freeman
Fresh-Beginnings

"Our mission is to foster confidence, independence, and self-esteem, enabling individuals to make healthy choices for themselves. By sharing our knowledge and encouraging others to try new foods and recipes, we hope to make mealtimes more enjoyable throughout the day. This book is all about simplicity. Our goal is to help people create delicious meals using ingredients they already have in their cupboards, while also encouraging the introduction of fresh, healthy, and nutritious options into their mealtimes."

"We all look for easy meal options, but it is important to ensure a healthy diet. This book not only offers some great recipes, but also some tips and information on how you can get the necessary confidence in the kitchen to help you to start providing enjoyable food and make healthy meals!"

"Wishing you all the very best on your journey and I really hope that you find this book useful."

Barbara

CONTENTS

Foreward	1
Welcome	2

Getting started

How to gain the confidence you need	6
Cooking from scratch	7
Healthy eating	8
Best before dates explained	8
Healthy eating guide	9
Tips for budgeting	10
Food safety & hygiene	11
Basic techniques	12
Batch cooking	13
Let's get cooking & be prepared	14
Sharpen your knives	14
Food for thought #1	15

Breakfast

To start your day off - Breakfast	17
Raspberry & Peanut Butter Smoothie	18
Breakfast Smoothies	18
Overnight Oats	18
All in One Breakfast ©ⓕ	19
Fruit Oats	20
Raspberry Oats	20
Quick & Easy Porridge	20
Easy Breakfast Omelette	21
Pancakes	21
Food for thought #2	22

Lunch

Sausage Rolls	24
Jacket Potatoes	25
Tuna Fish Cakes	26
Spicy Vegetarian Bean & Rice Bowl	27
Why buy canned tomatoes	27
Chicken & Vegetable Soup	28
Easy Homemade Tomato Soup	28
Lentil Soup	28
Quick Chilli Con Carne Nacho's	29
Sausage Fried Rice	30
Mushroom Carbonara	30
Chicken Fajitas	31
Food for thought #3	32

Dinner

Easy Pizza	34
Tuna Pasta Bake	35
Baked Lasagne	36
Cottage Pie ©ⓕ	37
Chilli Con Carne & Rice ©ⓕ	38
Chicken & Pea Risotto ©ⓕ	39
Chicken Curry ©ⓕ	40
Fish Pie ©ⓕ	41
Sausage & Mash Pie	43
Vegetable Casserole	43
Spaghetti Bolognese ©ⓕ	44
Easy Creamy Chicken Lasagne	45
Food for thought #4	46

Desserts

Home-made Ice-cream	48
Fruity Flapjack	48
Strawberry Mousse	48
Apple Crisp Crumble	49
Microwave Mug Cake	50
Home-made Custard	51
Baked Rice Custard	51
Rice Pudding Ice-cream	52
Shortbread Biscuits	52
Food for thought #5	53

Little Extras

Bread Rolls made from a Bread Mix	55
Healthy Tomato Ketchup	55
Garlic Bread	56
Home-made Baked Beans	56
Home-made Jacket Wedges or Chips	57
Basic White Sauce	57
Food for thought #6	58

Slow Cooker

Making the most of a slow cooker	60
Should you brown your meat first?	61
Slow Cooker Porridge	62
Slow Cooker Full English Breakfast	62
Slow Cooker Bolognese	63
Veggie Slow Cooker Curry	63
Slow Cooker Pizza	64
Slow Cooker Whole Chicken	64
Food for thought #7	65

Batch Cooking

Batch Cooking	67
Base Recipe for Mince	68
Base Recipe for Chicken in a White Sauce	68

Testimonials	70
Acknowledgements	71
& Finally	72

Recipe Variations
© Canned Version
ⓕ Fresh Version

GETTING STARTED?

"How to gain the confidence you need..."

Take a deep breath and take one step at a time. Creating your favourite dish is not a race or a competition – it should be an enjoyable experience and one of which you will be proud of!

Once you get cooking you won't look back. Start simple and expand as you become more adventurous as you gain in confidence – and YOU WILL!

Start with some simple recipes with not too many ingredients and learn how to cook them first. You will see as you learn to cook the basics and grow in confidence that you will be cooking your favourite recipes in next to no time.

So here we go!

Cooking from scratch is far cheaper than buying prepared meals - and much healthier too!

Putting this into practice can be a little scary, but don't worry - practice makes perfect.

As long as it tastes good and is edible, then your efforts will have paid off. You will improve as you gain more confidence and try new recipes.

Planning is the key ingredient. Check your recipe and make a list of what ingredients you need. Don't rush this as this is when mistakes can happen. It is all about the planning and preparation.

Before you rush out to buy ingredients, check what you have in your cupboards, fridge and freezer first, so that you are not buying items that you already have.

Cooking from scratch

What are the benefits of cooking from scratch?

Cooking from scratch is healthier, gives you control over what portions to use. You get to choose the ingredients, so you know what you are eating!

It is healthier
Ready-made meals and take-aways may be more convenient but they are anything but healthy. They are cooked with bad fats, sugar, and chemicals. These are cheap ways to make food taste better and the chemicals allow a longer shelf life, but they are not good for your health!

It saves money
A home-made meal is a much better alternative, and much more affordable. You will be pleasantly surprised how much money you save preparing your own food rather than spending it on ready-meals and take-aways.

Better tasting and enjoyable foods
Nothing compares to homemade cooked food because of the quality and freshness of the ingredients. After cooking your own meals, you will notice the different flavours and ingredients and you will realise just how good you are at cooking.

Better control
You will be in control of what you are eating, what the ingredients consist of and how much you eat – portion control!! You can make your favourite meals, repeatedly.

Family time
It brings families together and is one of the best benefits from cooking from scratch – cooking together and eating together.

Final thoughts: -
Cooking from scratch is fun, creative, therapeutic, and challenging – are you ready for it? You may not enjoy cooking – but once you get going and see the results you will realise how easy it is – you will learn to love it!!

Healthy eating

Healthy eating – what does it mean?

Healthy eating means including more fresh fruit and vegetables and cutting back on things like fried food, biscuits, salt, and sugary drinks. This will help you achieve and stay at a healthy weight.

Why healthy eating is important?

A healthy diet is essential for good health and nutrition. It protects you against many diseases, such as heart disease, diabetes, and cancer. Eating a variety of foods and consuming less salt and sugar are essential for a healthy diet.

What are the healthy foods to eat every day?

The basis of a healthy diet
- Eat plenty of colourful vegetables.
- Include legumes/beans in your recipes.
- Eat fruit.
- Introduce grain (cereal) foods – mostly wholegrain and high fibre varieties.
- Use lean meats and poultry, fish, eggs, tofu, nuts and seeds.
- Include milk, yoghurt, cheese or their alternatives, mostly reduced fat.
- Drink plenty of water.

Best before dates explained

Best before and use by dates – both quite different!

Understanding 'Best Before' and 'Use By' dates on food labels and how you must treat them differently.
Date marking - most pre-packed food comes with a date mark on the label:

Use-By Date
The most important date to remember is the Use-By Date

These dates are typically found on refrigerated goods, on perishable, high-risk food, such as meat, fish and dairy products that require chilled storage and have a short shelf life.
After the Use By date, do not eat it, cook it, or freeze it. The food could be unsafe to eat or drink, even if it has been stored correctly and looks and smells fine.

Best-Before Dates
These dates appear on less perishable food that has a long shelf life, such as canned, dried, and frozen products.
Best-before dates indicate the length of time for which a food will be at its best quality.
Food that has passed its best-before date is not unsafe to eat, but it may lose some of its flavour, texture, and quality.

Healthy eating guide

The Eatwell Guide shows the proportions in which different types of foods are needed to have a well-balanced and healthy diet. The proportions shown are representative of your food consumption over the period of a day or even a week, not necessarily each mealtime.

Some of the most important features of a healthy diet included in the Eatwell Guide are:

- Eat at least 5 portions of a variety of fruit and vegetables every day. This can include fresh, canned, or frozen fruit and vegetables. A typical serving of fruit is 80g of, but you can check on the label how many servings are in a can. Fruit and veg should make up just over a third of the food we eat each day
- Have two portions of sustainably sourced fish every week. You can usually see if the fish is responsibly sourced by checking the label. Oily fish such as mackerel, sardines, salmon, and pilchards contain particularly healthy fats called omega 3 fats. Make sure one of your weekly portions of fish is an oily fish.
- Pulses like lentils and beans can be a great source of vegetable protein and are high in healthy fibre. Include these in your diet. Pulses can count for up to one of your servings of vegetables each day.
- Some healthy fats are important for our bodies and brain. Oily fish, nuts, seeds, and some vegetables such as avocados are good sources of healthy "unsaturated" fats. Reduce the amount of saturated fats (found in butter, cheese, and meats) in favour of unsaturated fats (found in vegetable oils and olive oil).
- Wholegrain bread, pasta and flour have more fibre and nutrients than their refined (white) equivalents. Choose these when possible.
- Keep hydrated by drinking 6 – 8 glasses of fluid each day. Water, lower fat milk, unsweetened tea, and coffee all count. Remember you may have to drink more on hot days or if you are exercising.
- Food's high in fat, salt, and sugars (such as crisps, biscuits, and fizzy drinks) should be considered treats and are not part of a healthy diet.

Cooking your own food is the best way to make sure you are eating healthily. Cooking from scratch can save money and also means you know exactly what is going into your food.

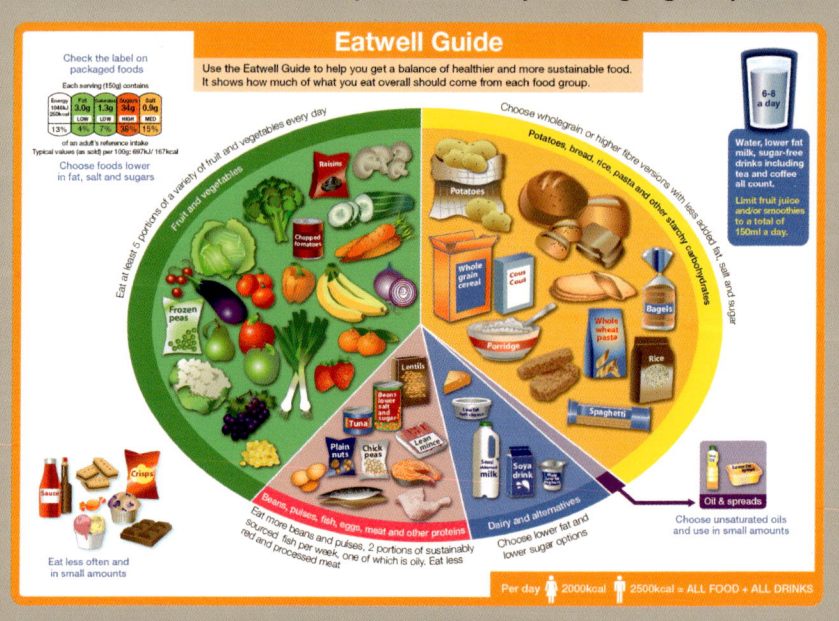

Tips for budgeting

If your budget is tight, it can seem difficult to buy foods that will help you have a healthier diet. Here are some tips that will help you reduce your shopping bill and eat more healthily at the same time.

Make a shopping list
This will help you to avoid buying additional items that you do not need.

Plan your meals for a few days ahead and make a list before you go shopping. Stick to the list when you are in the shop so that you don't buy additional items. Never shop when you are hungry - it always makes you buy extra!

Go for value
Buy the supermarkets' own brands – these are often cheaper and just as good quality.

Buy additional store cupboard items when they are on offer
Foods such as rice, pasta, cereal and canned foods will keep for a long time in your cupboard. Look for 2 for 1 offers and use these items to plan your next set of meals. Remember, except for the items on offer, stick to your shopping list!

Use frozen and tinned fruit and vegetables
These count towards your 5 a day. They may cost less than fresh and will not go off as quickly. In this way, you are less likely to have any waste and will save money.

Look for the supermarkets reduced item section
All supermarkets generally reduce the price of foods that are close to their use by date. This can be a great way to save money. Make sure you can use them before the date runs out and cook or freeze everything before it goes off.

Make your own meals
Cook your own meals – in this way you know what you are eating. Ready meals can be high in fat, sugar and salt. Cooking for yourself can be a lot cheaper and healthier!

Packets
Pasta, rice, and couscous all make great meals. Follow the instructions on the packets.

Jars
If you don't have the confidence to make your own sauces, there are a variety of different ones you can buy, such as curry or tomato, which will help you make some delicious meals. Making your own is a lot cheaper and healthier. (See further on in the book for recipes)

Cans
Tuna and salmon are great to mix with pasta and rice. Also, chopped tomatoes are good for making a quick pasta sauce. Look out for the varieties with added garlic or herbs. Don't forget everyone's favourite: baked beans, which can be eaten with any meal.

Finally
it is important to eat a healthy meal. If you are struggling to cook and have a cupboard full of cans and dried foods, it is amazing what you can make with a little imagination and the help offered in this book!

Food safety and hygiene...

"Number one in cooking!"

We all want to keep our families safe and healthy. Follow these tips for good food safety in the home.

Washing your hands
This might sound obvious, but it is crucial as germs on your hands can get into the food and make it unsafe.
- Wash your hands with soap and running warm water.
- Wash your hands before, during and after preparing food, before eating and after using the toilet.

Keep your equipment clean
- Use separate chopping boards, plates, and knives for different types of produce and for raw meat, poultry, fish, and eggs
- Make sure all your chopping boards, utensils and work surfaces are clean and kept clean in between preparing different foods.

Food preparation
- Do not wash raw meat, chicken or eggs. Washing these foods can spread germs as the juices or splashes from the water can land on your sink and counter.
- Do wash all fruit and vegetables under running water even if you are not going to peel them. Germs can spread from the outside to the inside as you cut or peel them.

Food safety – points to help keep you to be in control.

Cooking
Make sure you cook food thoroughly to a safe temperature. You must make sure that food is cooked for long enough, gets hot enough, and reaches a temperature of at least 72c

- When checking the temperature make sure you test the thickest part of the meat. If you don't have a probe, check carefully to see that the juices run clear.
- Do not put cooked meat back on a plate that has had raw meat on it – always use separate plates to avoid cross-contamination
- Do not leave foods out at room temperature any longer than 2 hours
- Cool hot food as quickly as possible. Divide roasts and large portions of food into small, lidded containers so that they will cool quickly. When cool place in the fridge or freezer.

Storage
- Keep your fridge temperature between 0c – 5c
- Keep your freezer temperature between -18c - -20c
- In order to avoid cross contamination, store raw meat on the bottom shelf away from fresh produce and ready to eat meals.
- Always keep food covered in lidded containers.
- Do not store opened cans of food in the fridge but transfer whatever is left to a plastic, lidded container.

Basic techniques

You do not have to become a professional chef or invest in lots of expensive equipment to cook healthier meals. Just look at some of the basic techniques below which will help you cook and prepare delicious and healthy foods.

No matter what you cook, you will still require healthy cooking methods to ensure you are looking after your health and nutrition and those of your family.

Baking
Baking is not for bread and cakes only. You can use this technique to cook almost anything: pieces of vegetable, fruit, seafood, poultry or lean meat.

Place food in a pan or dish. You may cook the food covered or uncovered, depending on what you are cooking. Baking generally doesn't require you to add fat to the food, so it makes it one of the healthier ways to cook.

Frying
This means cooking your food in fat. There are several variations of frying:

- Deep-frying, where the food is completely immersed in hot oil
- Stir-frying, where you fry the food very quickly on a high heat in an oiled pan
- Pan-frying, where food is cooked in a frying pan with oil
- Sauteing, where the food is browned on one side and then the other with a small quantity of fat or oil.

Frying is one of the quickest ways to cook food, with temperatures typically reaching between 175°C – 225ºC

Roasting
Roasting is basically just like baking, but at a higher temperature. It is a longer cooking process where hot air surrounds the food and cooks it evenly on all sides, browning as it cooks.

Braising
This technique consists of browning the ingredient in a pan on top of the cooker hob, then slowly cooking it with a small quantity of liquid for a long time until tender. Pot roasts, stews and casseroles can be cooked in this way if they contain larger food items such as poultry legs.

Grilling
Grilling involves cooking food on a rack with an overhead direct heat. Direct heat quickly sears the outside of food, producing distinctive, robust, roasted and sometimes pleasantly charred - flavours and a nice crust. Grilling allows fat to drip away from the food, making it one of the healthiest cooking methods.

Stir-frying
Stir-frying quickly cooks small amounts of food while they are stirred in a wok or a large non-stick frying pan. You need only a minimal amount of oil to prepare a healthy, quick meal.

Batch cooking

What are the benefits of batch cooking?

Batch cooking is a great technique which can save you time and money! Spend less time in the kitchen through the week by planning meals and reducing waste. Batch cooking ensures you always have a meal in your fridge or freezer – ready in minutes at the press of a button!

Lets get ready

One of the best ways to get started is to plan a base recipe – one that you can adapt for different dishes. Once made you can divide these into portions and freeze them in lidded containers so that you can enjoy them later, giving you a night off from cooking!

Plan what you are going to cook
Check your freezer first to see what room you have and what is already in there, so that you have a selection of meals to choose from. Make sure the recipes that you are choosing are suitable for freezing. Most are, except for egg - and cream-based sauces.

Make sure the recipes that you are choosing are suitable for freezing
Most are, except for egg and cream-based sauces.

Prepare your ingredients
As with all recipes, weighing and preparing your ingredients will make cooking so much easier.

Clean as you go
Cleaning as you go will help you stay in control of your kitchen. Always keep your work surfaces clean. Washing as you go will definitely help. No one wants to face a huge pile of washing and clearing up at the end!

Cool before you freeze
Once your recipes are ready, it is important that you cool them completely in their containers before freezing. Make sure you label and date your food before freezing as it is so easy to forget what it is and not easy to identify when frozen. **Check out the recipes for ideas on batch cooking (page 65).**

"Let's get cooking and be prepared..."

First, you will have chosen your recipe and you should by now have checked what ingredients and tools you need.

Clear a workspace in your kitchen to prepare your food. Give it a good wipe clean, preferably with a disinfectant spray before you put the food and utensils on it.

Get all your tools together and make sure they are clean and in working order ready for use. Make sure your knives are sharp and ready to use.

Check your recipe and always be sure to read it all the way through, not just the first instruction or two! Look at the ingredients, cooking times and what utensils you may need. Get all your ingredients together to ensure that you have everything required.

Take out of the fridge in advance your butter, eggs etc. so they can be brought to room temperature if your recipe requires this.

If you are using your oven, preheat this at the correct stage in the proceedings according to the recipe.
Weigh out all your ingredients and line them up in the order that the recipe tells you to use them.

"Clean as you go"

It is very important to clean as you go when cooking in a kitchen

- Keep worktops and chopping boards clean as they come into contact with the food you are going to eat.
- As you prepare food, get rid of debris and dirty pots as you go leaving your workspace clean and tidy - have a bowl ready for all your peelings, rubbish, and waste – this will help you to clean as you go, making it much easier to tidy up at the end.
- Fill your sink with hot soapy water so that you can put any dirty pots in to soak if you haven't got time to wash them as you go.

Sharpen your knives
Simply use an everyday household object.

Some people do not have a knife sharpener. If you don't, look no further – the solution is right here! You can sharpen any blunt knife by using a coffee mug, or possibly a coffee cup. Hold the mug firmly upside down in order to use the unglazed edge at the bottom. Take the knife you want to sharpen and, laying it flat on the base of the mug, slide it across the edge in a rapid motion 10 – 15 times. Do this for both sides of the knife. If still not sharp enough, repeat the process until it is.

Wash the knife before use.

It is important to keep your knives sharp. You will find that you'll have better control over what you do if you use a sharp knife rather than a blunt one. You will also need to apply more downward pressure if you use a blunt knife and, as a consequence, this will put you more at risk of personal injury.

Food for thought

Understanding your basic store ingredients

Non-perishable food items are those with a much longer shelf life and do not need refrigeration. The great thing about non-perishable foods is that you can buy them in advance and store them for much longer periods of time. It is always a good idea to have in a good supply to be used as part of your everyday cooking.

Keeping these items in stock will help you save time and effort the next time someone asks: "What's for dinner?" In addition to your canned and non-perishable foods, it is also helpful to have 'basic kitchen ingredients' in your cupboard where possible.

'Basic food suggestions...'

Using one or more of the items below, you can make a meal out of any of your canned and non-perishable foods.
Onions – they make food taste better.

Potatoes – these can be eaten mashed, boiled, roasted, baked, in a salad or as chips.

Seasoning – salt and pepper bring out the flavour of the food.
Cooking oil – rapeseed, sunflower, vegetable, or olive oil.

Bread – a particularly good filler! Choose wholemeal where possible. To save waste, keep in the freezer and use a slice at a time.

Flour – plain or self-raising flour – for sauces and baking.

Fresh vegetables – it is always good to have in fresh vegetables. They can be bought at a reasonable cost if you look around and look out for special offers.

A few kitchen essentials, to make things taste good:

Salt and pepper
A little sugar
Onions and garlic
Lemon juice
Vinegar
A few spices / garlic granules / dried herbs
Mustard
Worcester sauce
Chilli sauce

"The easiest way to start eating healthier is by preparing your own meals with fresh products"

BREAKFAST

To start your day off - Breakfast
How do you like your eggs fried or boiled?

Eggs really do make breakfast – they are great in so many ways

- They are inexpensive
- They are easy to prepare
- They cook quickly
- They are a good source of protein

Hard Boiled
A hard-boiled egg is cooked in its shell in boiling water. Keep it simple. Fill a pan with enough water to cover your eggs by about two inches. Bring it to the boil and carefully drop in the eggs leaving them for 10-12 minutes. For easier peeling after boiling, place the eggs immediately under a cold running water tap until they are cool, then gently tap and roll them on a counter before peeling.

Soft Boiled
Soft- boiled eggs follow the same process as hard-boiled eggs, but you cut the cooking time roughly in half. This means the egg white will be cooked while leaving the yolk runny. Soft- boiled eggs can be eaten in the shell, stood upright in egg cups. You can then daintily tap the top of the egg with a spoon and scoop out the insides. They are also great on toast or made into soldiers and dipped in the runny egg!

Scrambled eggs
Beat your eggs with a little milk in a separate bowl. Heat a knob of butter in a pan no higher than medium, pour the eggs in and keep gently stirring and folding the mixture while it cooks. Use a spatula to prevent them from spreading out, especially up the sides of the pan. Have your plate ready so you can remove them from the heat immediately. They are perfect on buttered toast with salt and pepper.

Poached eggs
Heat your water in a pan just shy of boiling point. Add a dash of vinegar! Crack the egg into a tiny bowl. Swirl the water in your pan to create a whirlpool, then carefully drop the egg into the centre. The swirling pulls the white together in the centre. Leave it in the water for about five minutes, then lift out with a slotted spoon.

Fried eggs – sunny side-up
Crack an egg directly into an oiled frying pan. As the yolk is runny, use a tablespoon to keep basting the egg. This will help the yolk cook. Depending on how long you fry it, the white of the egg is completely or partially set. If you like a harder egg, then you can use the spoon to flip it over (sunny side-down) just for a minute or two!

Tip!
To test an egg for freshness, place it in a glass of cold water.

If the egg sinks it is fresh!
If the egg floats – bin it!

Breakfast Smoothies

Make up a breakfast smoothie in next to no time. Use a banana with other soft fruit and add a little honey for sweetness – add a few oats for some additional fuel to get you through the morning to help you avoid snacking!

Ingredients:
- 1 banana
- 1 tbsp porridge oats
- 80g soft fruit - whatever you have – Fresh, frozen, or canned all work well.
- 150ml milk
- 1 tsp honey
- 1 tsp vanilla extract

Method:
Put all the ingredients in a blender and mix for 1 minute until smooth.

Pour the banana oat smoothie into two glasses to serve.

SERVES 1

Raspberry and Peanut Butter Smoothie

Ingredients:
- 1 x 300g Tin Raspberries
- 4 tbsps. Peanut Butter
- 2 tbsps. Oats
- 1 Litre Milk (any will do)

Method:
Whiz all the ingredients together until smooth

Chill or drink straight away.

SERVES 6

Overnight oats
Can be served in a variety of different ways!

Mix some oats and milk together with a yoghurt and a couple of your favourite ingredients and store in the fridge overnight for a healthy easy breakfast. You can get up and eat it – or it is good for on the go too!

Ingredients:
- 90g oats
- 300ml of any available milk (semi-skinned is better for you).
- 4 tbsp plain yoghurt (you can use flavoured – just not quite as healthy!).
- 1tsp vanilla extract (optional)
- 2 tbsp honey

Instruction:
Put all the ingredients in a bowl together and mix well.

Divide between individual bowls/containers and cover. Put in the fridge overnight for at least 6 hours.

Add whatever toppings you like -

Suggested toppings: -
1. Canned or fresh fruits
2. Canned or frozen berry mix
3. Mixed nuts
4. Dried fruit

SERVES 1

Did you Know

Juicing fruits & vegetables is healthy & refreshing - a great way to start your day!

Fresh juice is full of nutrients & can be very beneficial to your health

Overnight oats offer a range of health benefits, due to their rich fibre and protein content.

All in one Breakfast – The canned version!
Why not create a great breakfast that is quick and easy to put together ready for any morning start!

SERVES 4

Ingredients:
- 1 x 400g canned baked beans and sausage
- 1 x 380g canned spinach, drained (Fresh is much nicer).
- 1 x 400g canned chopped tomatoes
- 1 x 285g canned button mushrooms, drained
- 1 onion, sliced
- 1 tbsp of dried mixed herbs
- 1 vegetable stock cube plus 50 ml water
- 4 eggs

Method:
In a lidded saucepan, warm a little oil and start to soften the onion.

Add in the mixed herbs and give it a good stir. Once the onion has softened, pour in the chopped tomatoes, crumble in the stock cube, add the water, stir again, and leave to simmer for 5 minutes.

Now add the canned baked beans and sausages, mushrooms and spinach and simmer again just for a minute.

Now making four little wells in the tomato mix, crack in the raw eggs, do not worry if they spill over a little.

Pop the lid on and simmer gently, this is just to cook the eggs, when they are at your desired consistency, serve immediately with some thick slices of toasted bread.

All in one Breakfast – One pan brunch recipe

SERVES 4

Ingredients:
- 4 sweet potatoes, washed and diced
- 2 yellow peppers, sliced
- 1 red onion, cut into wedges
- 2 tbsp olive oil
- ¼ tsp paprika
- ¼ tsp ground cumin
- ¼ tsp chilli powder
- 400g tin chopped tomatoes
- 4 rashers smoked back bacon, fat removed, roughly chopped
- 50g baby spinach
- 4 eggs
- Fresh coriander, finely chopped, to serve (optional)

Method:
1. Preheat the oven to gas 6, 200°C, fan 180°C. Put the sweet potato, peppers, and onion in a large non-stick roasting tin. Drizzle with the oil, scatter over the spices and toss to coat, season. Bake for 15 mins, then add the tomatoes and bacon; bake for a further 15 mins.

2. Stir through the spinach, then make 4 wells, and crack an egg into each. Return to the oven and bake for 4-5 mins or until the spinach is wilted and the egg white is set but the yolks are still runny. Scatter over the coriander(optional)and spoon onto plates.

Fruit oats with rice pudding and honey

SERVES 2-4

Ingredients:
- 1 x 400g can rice pudding
- 200g oats
- 1 x 298 can of mandarins drained and chopped
- 50g mixed dried fruit (optional)
- 50ml milk – drizzle of honey

Method:
Mix the rice pudding with the oats and milk – layer it into bowls with the mandarins and mixed fruit, keeping some of the oat mixture for the top and drizzle with a little honey.

Raspberry oats

SERVES 2-4

Ingredients:
- 200g porridge
- Can raspberries and the juice
- 200ml milk - drizzle of honey

Method:
Put the oats in a bowl with the raspberries and juice (no need for overnight soaking or cooking). Add extra milk depending on how you like the consistency of your oats. Add honey.

Quick and easy porridge!

SERVES 1

Ingredients:
- 45g porridge
- 120ml water or milk or a combination of both.
- Toppings of your choice - maple syrup, golden syrup, honey, chopped fruit, dried fruit, sugar, cinnamon, or anything else you like

Even a couple pieces of chocolate!

Method:
Measure out your porridge quantity 45g and put into a large microwaveable container.

Add the water, milk or a 50/50 combination of the two.

Place into the microwave uncovered and set your timer for high for a couple of minutes.

Stir

Microwave for another 1 to 2 minutes, keeping an eye on the porridge to make sure it doesn't rise over the edge of the bowl.

Remove from the microwave and leave it to settle for a couple of minutes, then add the toppings of your choice.

You may need to add a little more liquid at the end if it becomes too thick and stodgy.

Easy Breakfast Omelette

SERVES 1

Ingredients:
- 2 eggs, beaten
- 60ml milk
- 1-2 tsp oil
- tsp butter

Method:
- Season the eggs with salt and pepper and beat well with the milk.
- Heat the oil and butter in a non-stick frying pan over a medium-low heat until the butter has melted and is foaming.
- Pour the eggs into the pan, tilt the pan ever so slightly from one side to another to allow the eggs to swirl and cover the surface of the pan completely.
- Cook for about 20 seconds then tilt the pan again to allow it to fill back up with the runny egg. Repeat once or twice more until the egg has just set.
- At this point you can fill the omelette with whatever you like – some grated cheese, sliced ham, fried mushrooms. Put the filling over the top of the omelette and fold gently in half with the spatula. Slide onto a plate to serve.

Pancakes

SERVES 2-4

Ingredients:
- 70g plain flour
- 2 eggs
- 100ml milk
- 1-2 tbsp oil

Method:
To make the batter, crack the egg into a large mixing bowl - add the flour, milk, and a tiny pinch of salt - mix everything together until you have a smooth batter - put a large frying pan on a medium heat and after a minute add ½ tablespoon of oil - add a ladle of batter to the pan, and swill it round the pan spread out slightly – each ladleful will make one pancake.

Cook the pancakes for 1 to 2 minutes, or until the bases are golden, then use a fish slice to carefully flip them over.

When the pancakes are golden on both sides, use a fish slice to transfer the pancakes to a plate. Serve with warmed marmalade or chocolate spread.

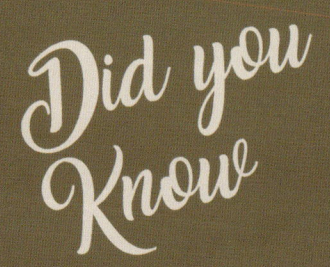

Did you Know

Apples are low in calories yet high in fibre & water, making them very filling & a great weight loss food!

Food for thought

Why use canned food?
The quality is great!

Cans go through an amazing process in a noticeably short time too so they can often retain the freshness and nutrient content, and in most cases, without the use of preservatives! Canned foods are more convenient as they do not go off the same as fresh foods. Canned foods can be a nutritious alternative when fresh foods are not available. Canned ingredients can be quickly adapted to make tasty recipes for families and individuals to enjoy.

Did you know?

Canned oily fish, such as sardines, pilchards and tuna, provides a good source of essential Omega 3. Fruit canned in juice provides one of your five-a-day. (Keep the juice from canned fruit, for example, raspberries, then add water to dilute it to taste. It makes a lovely refreshing drink!)

With a little bit of creativity, you can make healthy, easy and delicious dinners from some basic pantry staples:
- Canned, root and starchy vegetables
- Canned and dried fruits
- Canned proteins (tuna, salmon, chicken, beans, lentils)
- Dry wholegrains (bread, crackers, pasta, quinoa, rice)
- Nuts, seeds, and nut butter
- Herbs, spices, and oil

Where possible, add fresh ingredients if you have them and if you don't, are not keen on or are allergic to certain ingredients, substitute them for something else!

Avoid processed foods... Consuming them in excess can cause a lot of chronic health problems, such as obesity, high blood pressure & heart disease

What condiment has the most kick?

Horseradish!

LUNCH

Sausage Rolls

Makes 10

Ingredients:
- 1 x 500g of bought fresh puff pastry or ready rolled.
- 8-10 pork sausages approx. 5oog
- 100g apple sauce
- 1 egg yolk
- 50g of sage & onion stuffing mix – depending on taste, add more if required.
- A little milk
- Seasoning

Method:

Preheat the oven to 220°C, (200C in a fan oven), Gas Mark 7.

Roll the pastry and cut down the middle lengthways.

Remove the skin from the sausages and place in a bowl with the apple sauce, stuffing mix and seasoning and mix well.

Divide the sausage meat in half and place down the middle of each length of pastry.

Mix the yolk and milk in a small bowl with a fork and brush down one side of the pastry. (not too much, you do not want the pastry to be too wet).

Roll the pastry around the sausage meat using the egg to seal the edges. Cut each piece into approximately 6 sausage rolls and place on a lightly oiled baking tray. Brush the tops with the rest of the egg mixture.

Bake for 20 mins or until golden and cooked through. Allow to stand for 5-10 minutes before serving..

There is nothing wrong with using shop bought pastry – especially if you are short of time!

Try these homemade sausage rolls with the homemade baked beans which you will find the recipe for in the extras section. A delightful combination and can be served for either lunch or dinner!

Jacket Potatoes

Always welcome when your cupboard is bare.

Preparing your jacket potato for either oven or microwave
- Wash thoroughly, but not scrub as you will remove the skin
- Prick the potato – This helps to release the steam and create a nice fluffy potato
- You can also coat your potato in a little oil and roll it in a little salt – This helps to make the skin all crispy and adds more flavour.

Jacket potatoes can be ready in minutes if you cook them in the Microwave – Place prepared jacket potato in microwave on high setting for 3 minutes (800-watt) and the turn the potato over for another 3 minutes until tender. Add an extra minute if needed. (Adjust the time according to your microwave setting).

However, if you have a little extra time, you can cook them in the oven 180c/gas4 to get a nice crispy skin. This would take about an hour to an hour and a half. A good compromise would be to cook the potato in the microwave until almost cooked and then pop it into a preheated oven to finish it off for approx. 10-15 minutes or until nice and crispy.

While your jackets are cooking you can prepare your toppings or simply use leftovers from your Chilli, Bolognese, or curries!

A great way to use any additional leftovers from your batch cooking!

Toppings

Tuna, pepper and red onion
Finely chop 1/2 a red onion and 1/2 a red pepper and place in a bowl with a small, tin of tuna, drained. Mix in some mayonnaise and seasoning. Divide the filling into two halves. Put one half on the jacket. Store the remainder in a sealed tub in the fridge and you could use that to put on a sandwich.

Beans and Cheese
Heat the baked beans. Grate a good amount of cheddar cheese. Split the potato, add some butter, and pour over the beans. Sprinkle the cheese on top and watch it melt into the beans.

Coleslaw
A healthy option. Prepare your jacket and simply open a tub of coleslaw.
Place on your jacket and serve.

Bacon and cheese
Crispy bacon rashers chopped into pieces mixed in with the potato.
Grate some cheddar cheese on the top and place back in the oven to melt.

Bolognese
When you are making a spaghetti Bolognese, make a little extra and keep in the fridge until the next day. Prepare your cooked jacket, reheat your Bolognese thoroughly and add to the jacket potato.
You could also grate some cheddar cheese on the top and put back in the oven to melt.
All the above would be nice served with some salad, lettuce, tomato, cucumber, chopped peppers and spring onion.

Tuna Fish Cakes

SERVES 2-4

Everyone loves a fish cake – give your fishcake an extra taste with this crunchy oat recipe.

Ingredients:
- 180g packet mash potato (use fresh potato where available)
- 145g tuna in brine water, drained.
- 3 spring onions, sliced or 1 small onion sliced thinly or chopped (optional)
- 198g sweetcorn, drained
- 150g oats
- 2-3 tbsp mayonnaise
- 1 egg beaten
- 2-3 tbsp oil
- Seasoning

Method:
1. Make the mash potato as per packet instruction or boil potatoes, drain and mash with a knob of butter when cooked.
2. Add spring onions, mayonnaise and sweetcorn to the hot mashed potato and stir until thoroughly mixed, then add the tuna and season to taste. Allow the mixture to cool slightly.
3. Make the fishcakes: Divide and shape the mixture into 4-6 thick flat cakes.
4. Put the beaten egg in a dish and the oats in another dish. Dip the fishcake in the egg on both sides and then place it in the oats, shaking off any access.
5. Place the fish cakes in the fridge for 20 minutes to help them firm up.
6. Cook the fishcakes: Heat the oil in a large frying pan, preferably non-stick. Add the fishcakes and cook over a medium heat for 4-5 minutes on each side or until well browned, turning them carefully with a fish slice and serve.

Any canned fish will do – do not worry about the bones as they have been softened through the canning process.

If you would like to make them extra healthy bake them in the oven instead of frying for 15 minutes 220c / gas 7

Spicy Vegetarian Bean and Rice Bowl

SERVES 4

Ingredients:
- 2 x 395g Taco mixed beans in a spicy tomato sauce.
- 400g chopped tomatoes
- 410g haricot beans
- Oil
- 200g cooked rice as per packet instruction
- 4 tortilla wraps

Sprinkle with grated cheese or crushed Dorito's on the top.

For an extra hot and spicy dish add some dried chilli flakes to the bean mix and serve with soured cream before sprinkling the cheese or crushed Dorito's.

Method:
1. Prepare the tortilla bowls. Preheat the oven to 180C/350F/Gas 4. Take a sheet of foil about 1 metre/40in long and scrunch it up into a ball about 10cm/4in in diameter. Place it in the centre of a large baking sheet.
2. Take a tortilla and brush the centre on one side with a little of the oil – this will help prevent it sticking to the foil. Drape the tortilla over the ball of foil, oil-side down, pinching and loosely pleating it to create a bowl shape. Bake for five minutes until the bowl shape is set and the tortilla is lightly crisped.
3. Take the tortilla out of the oven and carefully remove it from the foil – it should be just cool enough to handle. Place the tortilla on an upturned tumbler and press to create a flat base on which to turn the tortilla once cold. The tortilla should still be warm enough to mould to the shape of the glass. Leave to cool while you make the next bowl in the same way. Put each upturned tortilla on a plate as soon as it is ready.
4. Cook the rice as per packet instruction and keep hot.
5. Put the canned ingredients in a pan and heat thoroughly.
6. Transfer the tortilla bowls to a dish and fill half full of rice and top with the spicy bean mix.

Why buy canned tomatoes?

Tomatoes packed in their juices can offer a fresher, fruitier flavour. They come in many different forms, such as whole, peeled, diced, stewed, crushed in puree, tomato paste and tomato puree. · Crushed tomatoes are a great base for a creamy tomato soup. · Diced tomatoes are a nice addition to chilli and curry. · Whole, crushed, or stewed tomatoes can be used to make a homemade pasta sauce. · Add tomato paste and/or diced tomatoes to homemade soups. Canned tomatoes are no substitute for fresh if you want to use them raw, such as in salads or in a sandwich.

Leftover Canned Tomatoes

If a recipe only needs half a can then put the leftovers in a non-metallic airtight tub in the fridge for up to 3 days or freeze.

Rinse those empty cans out.

If a recipe using canned tomatoes needs extra liquid or stock, then pour it into the can and give it a good swish round before adding. Remember, a good chef wastes nothing with flavour!

Don't forget to recycle those cans too!!

Recycling tips –
- Did you know that you need to wash items before they go into a recycling bin?
- Check if the items can be recycled by looking on the back of the packaging

Chicken and Vegetable Soup

SERVES 4-6

This is a very warming, easy chicken soup which makes the most of leftover roast chicken.

Ingredients:
- 55g butter
- 2 onions, sliced
- 2 sticks celery, finely chopped
- 2 carrots, finely diced
- 2 potatoes diced small
- 1 leek sliced thinly
- 25g plain flour
- 1.2 litres chicken stock
- 450g cooked chicken, skinned and shredded
- 1 tbsp chopped fresh parsley
- Salt and freshly ground black pepper

Method:
1. Melt the butter in a large saucepan over a medium heat and gently fry the onions, celery, potatoes, leek and carrots until they start to soften.
2. Stir in the flour and cook for 2 minutes. Add the chicken stock and bring the mixture to the boil, stirring as you do so.
3. Season with salt and pepper, then reduce the heat until the mixture is simmering and simmer for 20 – 25 minutes, or until the vegetables are tender.
4. Add the cooked chicken and cook until heated through. Adjust the seasoning, stir in the parsley, and serve.

Easy Homemade Tomato Soup

SERVES 4

This is one of the easiest, tastiest soups you can make. Store in the fridge for up to 3-4 days in a lidded container and heat as required.

Ingredients:
- 1 x 400g can chopped tomatoes
- 1 x 400g can carrots, sliced or diced
- 1 x 385g can apples, diced or pureed
- 1 x 500g jar or tub passata with a hint of chilli
- 1x 170g can evaporated milk (optional)

Method:
Put all your ingredients into a pan and heat gently. Add the evaporated milk to give it a creamy taste at the end. Ensure soup is piping hot and serve!

Lentil Soup

SERVES 4

Ingredients:
- 2 litres vegetable stock
- 150g red lentils
- 6 carrots, finely chopped
- 2 medium leeks, sliced
- Small handful of chopped parsley, to serve

Method:
Heat the stock in a large pan and add the lentils. Bring to the boil and allow the lentils to soften for a few minutes.
Add the carrots and leeks, and season. Bring to the boil, then reduce the heat, cover and simmer for 45-60 mins until the lentils have broken down.

Serve with your very own homemade bread rolls made from a bread mix – see the little extras section!

Quick Chilli Con Carne Nacho's

SERVES 2-4

If you are looking to spice up your lunch a little, look no further. These nachos are delightful, and you get extra carbs with the beans!

Ingredients:
- 1 x 400g can chilli con carne mince (or vegetarian option)
- 1 x 400g can chopped tomatoes drained
- 1 x 400g can mixed beans, drained and rinsed
- 1 x 180g packet tortilla crisps (or the equivalent)
- 1 x 40g packet cheese sauce

Method:
1. Preheat the oven to 180c / fan 160c gas 4.
2. In a bowl mix the chilli con carne mince with the beans and tomatoes.
3. Make up the cheese sauce according to instructions on packet, reducing the liquid a little as you need a slightly thicker sauce.
4. Put half of the tortilla crisps, layered, in an oven baked dish. Spread half the chilli con carne mix evenly over the top. Next drizzle half the sauce over the top, and then repeat.
5. Bake for 10 minutes.

Recipe Tips...

- This is a great recipe to use up homemade Chilli (see Mains recipes)
- If you have soured cream, you can use that instead of the cheese sauce packet
- If you have a salsa sauce you can add that instead of the tomatoes.
- You can spice it up by adding extra Chilli powder or grating a fresh Chilli on the top (or dried Chilli flakes - but go easy, especially if you are using the salsa sauce!)
- You can replace the mixed beans with chickpeas for a change

Sausage Fried Rice

SERVES 2-4

Sausage fried rice is a savoury egg fried rice dish that's quick and easy to make and can be on the table in less than half an hour.

We've used pouches of express cooked rice which just need heating through for a few minutes. Although they are a little pricier than cooking rice from scratch, it's worth keeping a few pouches in the store cupboard just for convenience. You can add some canned sweetcorn or frozen mixed vegetables to make the dish go further.

If you like, serve with extra soy sauce or a drizzle of sweet chilli sauce and some crispy prawn Chinese crackers.

Ingredients:
- 1½ tbsp sunflower oil
- 1 garlic clove, peeled and crushed
- 1 bunch spring onions, trimmed and finely chopped
- 2 thin spicy cooked sausages such as Pepperami, sliced
- 150g cooked chicken, finely chopped
- 2 x 250g pouches express long grain rice (use supermarkets own brand)
- 2 eggs, lightly beaten
- 2tbsp light soy sauce
- Salt and freshly ground black pepper

Method:
1. Heat the oil in a large frying pan until almost smoking. Add the garlic and spring onions and stir fry for 1-2mins. Add the sausage and chicken and stir-fry for a further 2-3mins.
2. Add the long grain rice and 3tbsp water and stir-fry over a medium-high heat for 4-5mins until piping hot.
3. Make a well in the centre of the rice mixture and add the beaten egg. Cook over a very high heat, stirring all the time until the egg has just set. Stir in the soy sauce and season lightly with salt and freshly ground black pepper. Serve immediately.

Mushroom Carbonara

SERVES 2-4

An easy, fuss-free way to create an 'Italian delight'. Pasta Carbonara is, without a shadow of a doubt, one of the most famous and representative dishes of the Italian culinary tradition. Enjoy!

Ingredients:
- 1 x 400g can of cream of mushroom soup
- 1 x 285g can of mushrooms, drained
- 2 x 200g tins of cooked ham, diced
- 1 x 410g can of garden peas, drained
- 400g dried spaghetti/tagliatelle
- Seasoning

Method:
1. Heat gently in a pan the mushroom soup, diced ham and peas, leaving them to simmer for 5 minutes.
2. Once the tagliatelle is cooked according to the instructions on the packet, stir in the sauce, mix well, and serve into bowls.

Recipe Tips...

- Swap the can of mushrooms for 250g fresh mushrooms, thinly sliced. Swap tin of cooked ham for bacon, diced small. Pan fry the bacon and mushrooms first in a little butter before adding to the soup).
- Pan fry some garlic and shallots, chopped with the mushrooms and ham.
- Instead of the soup, mix 3 eggs with a little cream, add to the mushroom mixture, mix well and then stir it in with your pasta.
- If you have any grated cheese add it to the ingredients when adding to the pasta. Stir well, but gently.
- Any pasta will work!

Chicken Fajitas

SERVES 4

Ingredients:
- 3 chicken fillets sliced
- 1 onion sliced into thin wedges
- 1 red pepper sliced
- 1 yellow or green pepper sliced

Marinade
- 4 tbsp oil
- 1 lime juiced
- 2 garlic cloves crushed
- 2 tsp paprika
- ½ tsp chilli powder
- 1 tsp oregano
- 1 pinch of ground cumin

To serve
- 4 tortilla wraps (instead of tortilla wraps you can use large lettuce leaves to make into a wrap).
- 1 bag fresh green mixed salad
- Tomato salsa (see additional recipe)
- 3 tbs half fat crème fraiche
- 150g grated cheese

Directions:
1. Slice the chicken breasts in half horizontally, then cut them into thin strips. Put them in a bowl, add the marinade ingredients and rub into the chicken with your hands.
2. Heat the oil in a large frying pan and fry the onion wedges until softened, add the peppers, cook them until soft, then transfer to a baking tray and keep warm.
3. Heat a little more oil in the frying pan and cook the chicken in batches over a high heat. Allow them to catch a little on the edges but don't overcook them. Add them to the baking tray to keep warm.
4. Heat the tortillas in a clean, hot frying pan, then wrap in foil and keep warm in the oven. Alternatively, heat in the microwave following pack instructions.
5. Make up the wraps with the salsa, chicken, onions and pepper and top with crème fraiche and grated cheese.
6. Enjoy!

Food for thought

Why drink water every day?

During everyday activities, water is lost by the body and this needs to be replaced. Your body needs water to help it work properly. If we do not drink enough water daily then we risk becoming dehydrated, which can cause serious health problems. Hydration is needed for digestion, for our heart and circulation, for temperature control and for our brain to work well.

Did you know?

Water is the healthiest choice for quenching your thirst, at any time – It has no calories, no caffeine and no sugars that can damage teeth.

Just how much water should we be drinking per day?

Drinking little and often is the best way to stay dehydrated NHS recommends 6-8 glasses daily.

More will be required in hot weather or when exercising.

'Recipe tips...'

- Choose water instead of sugary drinks.
- Add fresh fruit – try crushing your favourite fruit and add it to your water. Cucumber and fresh mint can be refreshing.
- Add juice – add natural juice with no added sugar such as cranberry, pomegranate, grape, or apple.
- Add a slice of orange, lemon, or lime to your water.
- Make sure your children are getting enough water too!
- Serve water during your meals.

Juicing vegetables is an excellent way to add more vitamins and minerals to your daily diet

Dark leafy greens like kale and rocket are powerful and full of vitamins

DINNER

Easy Pizza

MAKES 1-2

You can't beat a great pizza – and this one is so easy and tasty!

Ingredients:
- 1 x 290g packet pizza mix, 100ml Lukewarm water, flour for rolling.
- 400g chopped tomatoes
- 1 tsp dried mixed herbs
- Tbsp tomato puree
- 2 pinches of sugar,
- 250g grated cheese
- Topping of your choice

Suggested toppings:
- Ham, diced bacon, or pepperoni
- Diced pineapple
- Diced BBQ chicken (mix cooked chicken with a little BBQ sauce)
- Tuna
- Sweetcorn
- Onions and peppers
- Tomatoes

Method:
1. Switch the oven on to 220c / fan 200c gas 7 and grease and lightly flour a baking tray.
2. Make pizza as per packet instruction.
3. To make the sauce put tomatoes, sugar, puree, and mixed herbs in a bowl and mix well – place in the fridge until required.

Now to get creative: -
1. Top your pizza with the tomato mix, not too thickly and then evenly spread the grated cheese.
2. Add the toppings of your choice.
3. Bake in the oven for 15 – 20 minutes until the edges are nicely browned.
4. Serve and enjoy!

Tuna Pasta Bake

SERVES 4-6

Ingredients:
- 500g pasta
- 100g frozen peas
- 50g butter
- 50g plain flour
- 600ml milk
- 1 tsp Dijon mustard
- 125g cheddar, grated
- 3 x 145g cans tuna, drained
- 4 spring onions, sliced
- 198g can sweetcorn, drained
- Seasoning

Method:
- Heat oven to 180C/fan 160C/gas 4.
- Bring a pan of water to the boil. Add the pasta and cook, following pack instructions, until slightly tender. Add the peas for the final 3 mins cooking time.
- Meanwhile, melt the butter in a pan over a medium heat. Stir in the flour and cook for 2 mins. Add the milk, whisking constantly, then slowly bring to the boil, stirring often, until sauce thickens. Remove from the heat, add the mustard and season well.
- Drain the pasta and peas, then return to the pan and stir in the tuna, spring onions, sweetcorn, and sauce. Tip into a shallow baking dish, season and top with the cheddar and bake in the oven for 15-20mins or until golden and bubbling.

Baked Lasagne

This is a family favourite comfort food – perfect on a cold night!

Ingredients:
- About 10 sheets lasagne
- Make up half quantity of mince base mince recipe (see batch cooking section)
- Make white sauce (see white sauce recipe in the extra section)

Method:
- Preheat the oven temperature to 200c / fan 180c gas 6.
- For the lasagne, put one third of the meat sauce in the base of a 2.3 litre/4-pint shallow ovenproof dish. Spoon one third of the white sauce on top. Arrange one layer of lasagne sheets on top. Season. Spoon half of the remaining meat sauce on top and then half of the white sauce. Put another layer of lasagne sheet on top, then the remaining meat sauce and remaining white sauce. Sprinkle over the cheddar cheese.
- Leave for a couple of hours to rest before cooking so that the pasta can start to soften.
- Cook in the middle of the oven for about 45 minutes- or until golden brown on top, bubbling around the edges and the pasta is soft.

Leave to rest for 15 – 20 minutes to help it set and keep it from being runny.

~

This lasagne freezes well. Just assemble it but do NOT bake. Instead, wrap the assembled lasagne tightly with plastic wrap, then wrap again with aluminium foil and freeze for up to 1 month.

Defrost over night in the refrigerator and then follow instructions as above.

Cottage Pie - Canned Version

SERVES 4

Ingredients:
- 2 x 400g tinned minced beef and onion
- 1 x 400g mixed vegetables drained
- 1 x 400g vegetable soup
- 1 x 180g instant mash
- 50g oats (optional)
- seasoning

Method:
- Switch oven on to 180c / fan 160c gas 4.
- Cook the instant mash according to instruction.
- Mix together all the ingredients and put into an oven proof dish.
- Add the mash to the top spreading it out with a fork.
- Sprinkle the top evenly with the oats.
- Bake in the oven for 20-30mins.
- When nicely golden, serve and enjoy!

Cottage Pie - Fresh Version

SERVES 4

Ingredients:
- Make up half mince base recipe, (refer to batch section)
- 750g potatoes, peeled and chopped
- 125g unsalted butter
- 150ml milk
- 200g grated cheese

Method:
- Preheat the oven to 200c / fan 180c gas 6.
- Tip the mince into an oven bake dish and set aside to cool while you make the mash.
- Half-fill a large pan with cold water. Add the potatoes and bring to the boil, then reduce the heat to a simmer and cook for about 15 minutes, or until the potatoes are very soft.
- Drain the potatoes well and add the butter, milk and cheese and mash until smooth and creamy. Season with salt and freshly ground black pepper.
- Spoon the hot mash over the top, fluffing the top with a fork. Scatter over a few dots of butter, and grated cheese, then place in the oven for about 20 minutes, until golden-brown and piping hot throughout.

Chilli Con Carne and Rice - Canned Version

SERVES 4

Ingredients:
- 2 x cans 392g chilli mince
- 1 x 400g can of kidney beans, drained
- 1 x 400g can of chopped tomatoes
- 300g rice, (cooked per packet instructions)

Method:
- Heat chilli mince, kidney beans and chopped tomatoes together.
- When heated thoroughly, serve on top of the hot cooked rice.

Chilli Con Carne and Rice - Fresh Version

SERVES 4-6

Ingredients:
- Half quantity of the mince base recipe, (refer to batch section)
- 1 tsp ground cumin
- 1 tsp ground coriander
- 1 tsp hot chilli powder
- 1 x 400g can kidney beans, rinsed well,
- 300g rice (cooked per packet instruction)
- Seasoning.

Method:
- Make up the mince base recipe. Add the spices to the mix and cook through.
- Stir in the kidney beans.

Both chilli recipes can be served either with just rice or baked tortilla bowls or a combination of both. Serve the salad on the side.
(To make the tortilla bowls, see Spicy Vegetarian bean and rice Bowl recipe in the lunch section.)

Easy Perfect Rice

You can use a mug to make sure you reliably use the right amount of water to cook your rice perfectly.

For fluffy rice, put one cup of white rice (75g per person) into a sieve and rinse under cold water until the water begins to run clear. Put the rice into a saucepan with two cups of cold water. Bring the water to the boil and cook for the time stated on the packet, or until softened and most of the water has been absorbed by the rice.

Drain the rice into a large sieve and rinse by pouring over a kettle of very hot water. Leave to drain well, then tip into a warm serving dish, add seasoning and a knob of butter and fluff up the rice and serve!

If you want to flavour your rice, cook it in chicken stock or add the flavour you want when you are cooking the rice.

Chicken and Pea Risotto – Canned Version

SERVES 4

Ingredients:
- 200g rice (arborio or basmati)
- 700ml chicken stock
- 92g can of chicken in white sauce
- 1 x 290g can peas drained
- 1 x 285g can mushrooms, drained and cut up small

Method:
- Cook the rice in ¾ of the stock for 15 minutes, stirring regularly.
- Add the chicken and cook for a further 5 minutes. Add the peas and mushrooms along with the remainder of the stock and cook for another 5 minutes until it has all been heated through and there is hardly any liquid left other than a slight sauce.
- Add seasoning if required and serve..

Chicken and Pea Risotto – Fresh Version

SERVES 4

Ingredients:
- 2 tbsp mild olive oil or sunflower oil
- 1 onion, cut in half, coarsely grated
- 2 garlic cloves, grated
- 250g arborio
- 1 litre chicken stock cube, made with 1 stock cube
- 100ml extra water
- 250g cooked leftover chicken, skin removed, cut into small pieces
- 200g frozen peas
- 75g Grana Padano or other hard Italian-style cheese, finely grated
- 25g butter
- Freshly ground black pepper

Method:
1. Heat the oil in a large, non-stick saucepan over a medium heat. Add the onion and garlic and fry for 2-3 minutes, stirring occasionally, until softened and just beginning to colour.
2. Add the risotto rice to the pan and stir well for 30-40 seconds, until the oil has coated the grains of rice.
3. Add all of the stock and bring to the boil, stirring well. Reduce the heat and simmer, uncovered, for 8-10 minutes, stirring frequently, until the rice is almost tender, and the risotto is creamy in appearance.
4. Stir in the water, the chicken, and the frozen peas, then continue to cook, stirring constantly, for a further 4-5 minutes, or until the chicken and peas are heated through and the rice is tender with a slight bite.
5. Remove the pan from the heat, then stir in the butter and cheese. Season with black pepper. Cover the pan with a lid and set aside for 5 minutes before serving.

Recipe Tips...

Grana Padano cheese is similar in taste and style to Parmesan, but it costs less, perfect for those on a budget.

Even though all the stock is added at once, it is still important to stir the risotto regularly as it cooks in order to achieve a creamy texture.

When does bread rise?

When you 'yeast' expect it!

Why did the orange stop rolling down the hill?

It ran out of juice!

Chicken Curry – Canned Version

SERVES 2-4

Ingredients:
- 1 x 400g can of chicken in white sauce
- 1 x 285g can mushrooms, drained
- 1 x 400g can mixed vegetables, drained
- 1 x 500g jar of curry sauce

Method:
- Mix all the ingredients together in a pan.
- Bring to the boil, stirring constantly.
- Leave to simmer for 5-10minutes.
- Serve with either rice or couscous.
- You can swap the tinned chicken for leftover chicken and the tinned vegetables for fresh.
- Lightly cook the vegetables before adding to the chicken and sauce.

Chicken Curry – Fresh Version

SERVES 4-6

Ingredients:
- 1 tbsp oil
- 650g boneless chicken thighs, cut into pieces
- 25 g butter
- 1 large onion chopped into small dice.
- 1 green pepper, cut into pieces.
- 2-3 garlic cloves, peeled
- 1 tsp ground ginger
- 1 tsp chilli powder
- 3 tsp garam masala
- 1 tsp coriander
- 2 tsp Ccumin
- 1 tsp turmeric
- 2 tsp curry powder
- 200 ml chicken stock
- 1 400 g tin chopped tomatoes.
- 2 tbsp tomato purée
- 1 tbsp. flour
- 1/2 tsp salt
- 1 tbsp brown sugar
- Chopped fresh coriander (optional)

Method:
1. Heat the oil in a large saucepan and add the chicken pieces. Cook over a high heat until the chicken has browned. Remove the chicken from the pan and set aside.
2. Melt the butter in the pan and add the onion, garlic, and ginger. Cook on a medium heat until it is beginning to colour and smells fragrant. Stir in the chilli powder, Garam Masala, turmeric, coriander, and cumin. Cook for one minute.
3. Gently add in the flour and mix and then add the chicken stock, mixing quickly and thoroughly.
4. Add in the chopped tomatoes, tomato purée, salt, and sugar. Bring to the boil, keep stirring gently.
5. Add the chicken pieces to the sauce, making sure the pieces of chicken are well covered with sauce.
6. Cover the pan loosely with a pan and leave to simmer for 20 – 30 minutes until tender.
7. Sprinkle with chopped fresh coriander and serve with rice, Naan bread, poppadoms, and mango chutney.

Once cooked, this curry can be stored in the fridge for up to 3 days. Reheat until piping hot before serving.

Fish Pie – Fresh Version

SERVES 4-6

Ingredients:
- 400g skinless white fish fillet
- 400g skinless smoked haddock fillet
- 600ml full-fat milk
- 1 small onion, quartered
- 4 cloves
- 2 bay leaves
- 4 eggs
- Small bunch parsley, chopped
- 100g butter
- 50g plain flour, pinch freshly grated nutmeg(optional)
- 1kg potato, peeled and cut into even-sized chunks
- 50g cheddar, grated

Method:
1. Poach 400g skinless white fish fillets and 400g skinless smoked haddock fillets. Put the fish in the frying pan and pour over 500ml of the full-fat milk. Quarter 1 small onion and stud each quarter with a clove, then add to the milk, with 2 bay leaves. Bring the milk just to the boil - you will see a few small bubbles. Reduce the heat and simmer for 8 mins. Lift the fish onto a plate and strain the milk into a jug to cool. Flake the fish into large pieces in the baking dish.
2. Hard-boil 4 eggs. Bring a small pan of water to a gentle boil, then carefully lower the eggs in with a slotted spoon. Bring the water back to a gentle boil, with just a couple of bubbles rising to the surface. Set the timer for 8 mins, cook, then drain and cool in a bowl of cold water. Peel, slice into quarters and arrange on top of the fish, then scatter over the chopped leaves of a small bunch of parsley.
3. Make the sauce. Melt 50g butter in a pan, stir in 50g plain flour and cook for 1 min over moderate heat. Remove from the heat, pour in a little of the cold poaching milk, then stir until blended. Continue to add the milk gradually, mixing well until you have a smooth sauce. Return to the heat, bring to the boil and cook for 5 mins, stirring continually, until it coats the back of a spoon. Remove from the heat, season with salt, pepper, and a pinch of freshly grated nutmeg(optional), then pour over the fish.
4. Assemble and bake. Heat oven to 200C/fan 180C/gas 6. Boil 1kg of floury potatoes, cut into even-sized chunks, for 20 mins. Drain, season and mash with the remaining 50g butter and 100ml full-fat milk. Use to top the pie, starting at the edge of the dish and working your way in. Push the mash right to the edges to seal. Fluff the top with a fork, sprinkle over 50g grated cheddar, then bake for 30 mins. Make up to a day ahead, chill, then bake for 40 mins.

Tuna and Salmon Fish Pie – Canned Version

SERVES 4

Ingredients:
- 1 x 25g packet white sauce mix
- 145g can tuna, drained
- 1 x 213g can pink boneless salmon, drained
- 1 x 290g can peas, drained
- 1 x 198g can sweetcorn and mixed peppers, drained
- 1 x 180g packet mash potato
- 50g oats
- Seasoning

Method:
Heat oven to 180c / fan 160c gas 4 – grease an oven proof dish – make sauce as per packet instructions – add tuna, salmon, peas, sweetcorn and peppers and gently mix together – season – put mixture in the oven dish. Make up mash as per packet instructions and spread carefully over the mix with a fork – sprinkle the oats over the top – bake in the oven for 25 – 30 minutes until thoroughly hot – serve and enjoy!

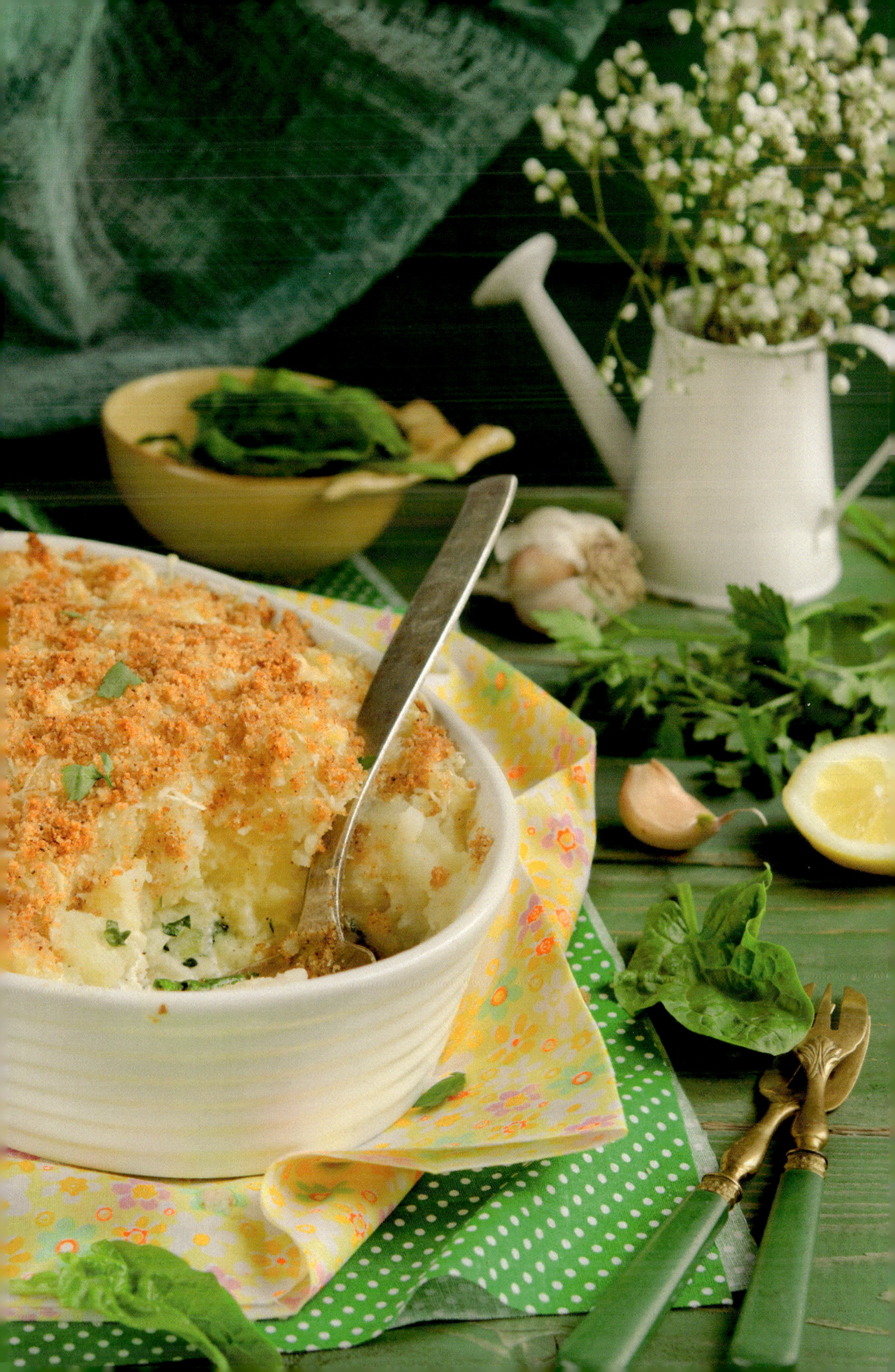

Sausage and Mash Pie

SERVES 6-8

Ingredients:
- 800g sausages (about 70g/2.5oz each)
- 1tbsp olive oil
- 1 onion finely sliced
- 10 mushrooms sliced
- 415g can baked beans canned
- 4 sprigs fresh thyme leaves only
- 2tbsp flour
- 550ml beef stock
- 1tsp Marmite
- 800g potatoes peeled and chopped
- 20g butter
- 4tbsp milk
- 1tbsp Dijon mustard
- 50g mature cheddar
- Seasoning

Method:
1. Add the potatoes to a pan of boiling water and boil until soft, about 15 minutes.
2. Heat the oil in a large pan and cook the sausages according to the packet instructions - usually 10-12 minutes. Once cooked, set aside.
3. Add the onion and mushrooms to the pan. Cook until softened, about 5 minutes. Add the flour, stock and Marmite. Simmer for a further 3 minutes.
4. Once the potatoes are cooked, drain and add the butter, milk and mustard. Mash until you get your desired consistency.
5. Chop the cooked sausages into bite-sized pieces and add to the pan of vegetables with the baked beans and thyme. Mix well and adjust seasoning if required.
6. Transfer to a large baking dish and place in a preheated oven 200c / fan 180c gas 6 for 20-30 mins
7. Spread the mashed potato over the top of the sausage mixture then sprinkle with grated cheddar. Cook in a hot oven 180c / gas 4 for 30 minutes until the cheese has melted.

Notes:
- If you are using sausages with a high fat content, you might not need to add any oil to the pan to cook them in.
- Make sure the baking dish you are using is big enough, so everything doesn't spill out when it's cooking in the oven.
- For a richer flavour, add a splash of red wine at the same time as the stock.
- Cool the meat mixture a little before adding the potatoes. This allows it to thicken up and makes it easier to spread the potatoes on top. The creamier the potatoes, the easier they are to spread.

Vegetable Casserole

SERVES 4

Ingredients:
- 2 tbsp oil
- 1 large onion, finely chopped
- 2 cloves garlic, crushed
- 2 carrots, chopped into small chunks
- 3 sticks celery, thinly sliced
- 1 sweet potato, peeled and chopped small
- 2 courgettes, chopped small
- 1 small aubergine, chopped small
- 1 litre vegetable stock
- 1 x 400g can chopped tomatoes
- 3 tbsp tomato puree
- 1 tsp mixed herbs
- 1 x 400g can kidney beans, drained
- Seasoning

Method:
1. Heat the oil in a large pan.
2. Add the onion and cook for a few minutes until soft.
3. Add the carrot, celery, sweet potato, aubergine and mixed herbs, mix well.
4. Add the garlic and cook for a couple of minutes.
5. Add the stock, tinned tomatoes and puree and stir well.
6. Bring to the boil and then turn down the heat and simmer gently for 15 minutes until the vegetables are just cooked. Stir from time to time.
7. Add the kidney beans and simmer for a few minutes until the beans are heated through.
8. Season to taste.

Recipe Tips...

You can add chicken to this recipe by frying off the meat first until browned. Transfer to another dish while you cook off the vegetables. Add the chicken back into the mix just before you add the stock. For more flavour you could add chicken stock in place of the vegetable stock.

Spaghetti Bolognese – Canned Version

SERVES 4

Ingredients:
- 2 x 392g cans Minced Beef & Onion
- 400g can chopped tomatoes
- 2 tbsp tomato puree
- 285g can mushrooms, drained and sliced
- 1 tsp dried Italian mixed herbs
- Salt and freshly ground black pepper
- 350g dried spaghetti

Method:
1. Empty the cans of Minced Beef & Onion into a large saucepan. Add the chopped tomatoes, tomato puree, mushrooms, and herbs. Heat and simmer for 20 minutes, stirring occasionally.
2. When the Bolognese sauce has been cooking for 10 minutes, put the spaghetti on to cook in a large saucepan of lightly salted boiling water. Cook according to pack instructions for around 10-12 minutes.
3. Drain the spaghetti and share between 4 serving plates or bowls. Season the Bolognese sauce and mix with the spaghetti and serve If you have any spare cheese in the fridge finish off by grating a little on top before serving!

Spaghetti Bolognese – Fresh Version

SERVES 4

Ingredients:
- 2 tbsp olive oil
- 500g beef mince
- 1 onion roughly chopped.
- 2 sticks celery, diced (optional)
- 2 carrots, finely diced
- 2 garlic cloves, crushed
- 200ml pint beef stock
- 2 tsp Worcestershire sauce
- 1 tbsp redcurrant jelly (optional) or 1 tsp caster sugar
- 2 tbsp tomato purée
- 1 tsp dried thyme
- 2 x 400g cans chopped tomatoes
- 2 bay leaves

Method:
1. Heat a large frying pan until hot and add the oil.
2. Cook the mince until browned all over. Remove from the heat and transfer to a plate.
3. Add the onion, carrot, celery (if using) and garlic to the pan. Cook until softened.
4. Return the meat to the pan and add the stock. Bring to the boil.
5. Add the redcurrant jelly (or sugar), tomato purée and thyme, then stir well.
6. Stir in the canned tomatoes. Bring to the boil again, cover and simmer for an hour and a half or until tender.

This can be served with any pasta of your choice. Finish off with a little grated cheese before serving!

For a richer flavour, add a splash of red wine at the same time as the stock.

Easy Creamy Chicken Lasagne

SERVES 4-6

Ingredients:

- About 10 lasagne sheets
- 36g packet cheese sauce mix (or use the white sauce recipe from the extras section)
- 2 x 392 g tinned chicken in white sauce (or use the chicken base recipe from the batch cooking section)
- 400g can chopped tomatoes with herbs, drained (reserve the liquid)
- 285g can mushrooms, drained and chopped into quarters
- 400g can mixed vegetables, drained
- 380g can spinach, drained thoroughly
- 1-2 packs cheesy tortilla crisps lightly crushed (or grated cheese)
- Seasoning

Method:

1. Preheat the oven temperature to 180c / fan 160c gas 4.
2. Cook sauce as per packet instruction.
3. Empty chicken in sauce into a bowl and gently using two forks loosen/flake the chicken.
4. Gently add to the chicken the chopped tomatoes, mixed veg and mushrooms and season to taste if required.
5. Slowly add the liquid you have kept from the tomatoes to the mix so that it forms a coating consistency – you do not want it too sloppy!
6. Add a layer of the mix into the dish and spoon small clumps of spinach on top. Place the lasagne sheets over the top, avoiding over laying. Cover lightly with the sauce and then repeat.
7. The top layer should be the cheese sauce. Season and sprinkle the tortilla crisps on the top. Cover with tinfoil for 30 minutes.
8. Remove tinfoil and bake for a further 5- 10 minutes until brown and bubbly.

Food for thought

Why use nuts and seeds?

Nuts and seeds are good sources of protein, healthy fats, fibre, vitamins and minerals. Nuts and seeds regulate body weight as their fats are not fully absorbed. They regulate food intake and help burn energy.

Did you know?

Nuts and seeds make up an important part of a healthy diet. Both types of food help you reach your recommended intake of protein each day, as well as counting towards your daily fat allowance. Seeds and nuts benefit your health because they offer key essential nutrients and play a role in disease prevention by keeping you healthy as you age.

'Recipe tips'

Store nuts and seeds in a cool, dry place away from heat and sunlight.

Most recipes ask for nuts and seeds to be roasted – why?

The process of roasting enhances their flavour. It draws out their natural oils, giving a rich nutty essence, creating a deeper colour and making them crunchier, thereby adding a whole new experience to their taste!

Strawberries have MORE vitamins than oranges!

ONE can of soda contains 10 tsps of sugar!

It takes 20 minutes for your brain to know that your stomach is full!

DESSERTS

Home-made ice-cream

SERVES 4

No ice-cream maker required!

Ingredients:
- 300ml double cream
- 3 eggs
- 70 g icing sugar
- 3 tbsp golden syrup

Method:
- Whisk the cream until it is thick (not too thick)
- Whisk in a separate bowl the eggs and icing sugar until it doubles in volume
- Add in the golden syrup
- Add the cream to the egg mixture and transfer to a lidded tub and Freeze

To make the ice-cream a little different you can add broken up pieces of crunchie (or whatever else takes your fancy) to the mix before freezing!

Fruity Flapjack

Flapjacks are deliciously sticky and are a perfect snack food. They keep well, and the oats are a good source of fibre, which slows the release of sugar into the body.

Ingredients:
- 175g Butter
- 175g Demerara Sugar
- 1 tbsp Honey or Golden Syrup
- 1/2 tsp Vanilla Extract
- 250g Rolled Oats.
- 100g Mixed fruit
- 50g Melted chocolate to drizzle on the top. (optional)

Method:
1. Grease and line a 20x20cm square tin. Preheat the oven to 180C/160Fan/350F.
2. Melt the butter, vanilla, sugar and honey or golden syrup in a large pan. Once the butter has melted and all the sugar has dissolved, tip in the oats and dried fruit and mix well.
3. Tip the mixture into the lined tin, press down evenly, and bake for 20-25 minutes for soft, chewy flapjacks. If you like a crispy flapjack bake for about 30 minutes.
4. When cooled drizzle some melted chocolate over the top for that extra little treat.

MAKES 8-10

Strawberry Mousse

MAKES 4

Ingredients:
- Strawberries, 225g
- 300ml Double Cream, a medium pot
- 1/2 lemon
- Icing Sugar, to taste

Instruction:
- Wash and remove the stalks from the strawberries.
- Crush the strawberries with a potato masher until you have a lumpy puree. If there is too much liquid, strain some away. This stops the cream from getting too runny.
- Whip the cream in the other bowl with the rotary whisk until, when you lift up the whisk, the cream forms little mountain peaks.
- Using a tablespoon, fold the crushed strawberries into the bowl of cream, using the spoon like a paddle, until the strawberries are all completely folded in and there is no more white cream. Add a squeeze of lemon juice, to taste.
- How much icing sugar you need, depends on how sweet you like it. Sift in a little, heaped spoonful at a time, folding it in well. Keep tasting the mixture, until it is exactly right.

Fun!

What is the most relaxing pasta?

Spa-ghetti!

What has a T in the beginning, in the middle, and at the end?

A Teapot!

48

Apple Crisp Crumble

MAKES 4-6

Ingredients:

For the Topping:
- 100g plain flour
- 150g cup packed light brown sugar
- Pinch of salt
- 110g unsalted butter (cold, cut into small pieces)
- 75g quick-cooking or rolled oats

For the Filling:
- 5 to 6 large apples
- 1 tablespoon lemon juice
- 75g cup packed light brown sugar
- 1/2 teaspoon ground sweet cinnamon

Method:
- Heat oven to 180C/160C fan/gas 4.
- Butter a 24cm/9in ovenproof dish.
- Combine the flour, 150g brown sugar, salt, and butter in a mixing bowl.
- Add in the butter to the dried ingredients and rub gently until it looks like breadcrumbs.
- Add the oats and mix thoroughly. Set aside.
- Peel, core, and slice the apples.
- Add the apple slices in a bowl with the lemon juice and toss periodically to keep the apples from becoming brown.
- Add the 75g brown sugar and cinnamon to the apple and lemon juice mixture and toss.
- Transfer the apple mixture to the prepared baking dish.
- Top the apple mixture evenly with the crumb mixture.
- Bake for 40 to 45 minutes, or until the apples are tender and topping is browned and crisp.

Microwave Mug Cake

Quick and simple microwave mug cake - all you need is a mug and a microwave!

Ingredients:
- 4 tbsp self-raising flour
- 4 tbsp caster sugar
- 2 tbsp cocoa powder
- 1 medium egg
- 3 tbsp milk
- 3 tbsp vegetable oil or sunflower oil, a few drops of vanilla essence or other essence (orange or peppermint work well)
- 2 tbsp chocolate chips, nuts, or raisins etc (optional)

Method:
- Add 4 tbsp self-raising flour, 4 tbsp caster sugar and 2 tbsp cocoa powder to the largest mug you have (to stop it overflowing in the microwave) and mix.
- Add 1 medium egg and mix in as much as you can, but do not worry if there's still dry mix left.
- Add the 3 tbsp milk, 3 tbsp vegetable or sunflower oil and a few drops of vanilla essence and mix until smooth, before adding 2 tbsp chocolate chips, nuts, or raisins, if using, and mix again.
- Centre your mug in the middle of the microwave oven and cook on High for 1½ -2 mins, or until it has stopped rising and is firm to the touch.

Recipe Tips...

As a general guideline, if you have a high wattage microwave the mug cakes will take less time to cook, so do experiment the first time you make them. Banana and honey are such a great combination for a mug cake. Sweet, smooth, and yummy, it is the perfect dessert that takes no time at all when using a microwave.

Home-made Custard

Ingredients:
- 600ml/1 pint full-fat milk
- 3 free-range eggs, yolks only
- 25g/1oz caster sugar
- 2 tsp cornflour
- 1 tsp vanilla extract

Method:
1. Heat the milk in a pan over a medium heat, stirring frequently, until just coming up to boiling.
2. Mix together the egg yolks, sugar and cornflour in a heatproof bowl stirring to get a smooth paste.
3. Slowly pour the hot milk into the paste, stirring constantly until completely combined.
4. Stirring constantly, cook gently over a low heat until the custard thickens – and serve.

Baked Rice Custard

MAKES 1

This is a favourite Australian dish, very tasty and can be served hot or cold!

Ingredients:
- 1 mug white rice cooked
- 1/2 mug sultanas or mixed fruit to taste
- 2 cups milk
- 1 x 170g can carnation evaporated milk (or cream)
- 60g caster sugar
- 3 eggs
- 1 tsp vanilla essence (optional)
- 1 pinch nutmeg (optional)

Method:
- Preheat oven to 200c / fan 180c gas 6.
- Lightly grease an ovenproof dish.
- Place dish into a larger dish filled with hot water. (Please be careful).
- Place cooked rice and sultanas into the greased dish.
- Whisk eggs in a large bowl with milk, evaporated milk or cream, sugar, and vanilla essence. Pour over rice and sultanas.
- Bake for 30 minutes, then stir gently with fork.
- Bake for a further 30 minutes, then stir and sprinkle with nutmeg.
- Bake for a further 20 minutes, or until custard has set.
- Serve hot or cold with topping of choice.

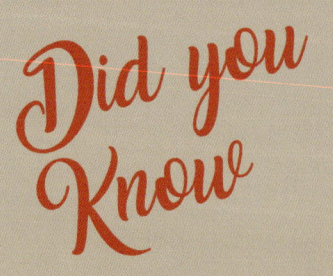

Did you Know

Carnation Evaporated Milk is the perfect creamy topping for all your favourite desserts from a fresh fruit salad to a sticky toffee pudding.

Made from fresh milk so it is a source of calcium and it's also fortified with Vitamin D; it is available in a light version which is less than half the fat of Carnation Evaporated Milk.

Rice Pudding Ice-Cream

Makes 1 Litre

Ingredients:
- 190g can rice pudding
- 300g can peach slices – drained
- 1 tsp of vanilla essence
- 500g natural yogurt, 20g sugar, shavings of white & dark chocolate
- Crushed ginger biscuits

Method:
1. Pour the natural yogurt and the sugar into a mixing bowl. Mix until the sugar has melted.
2. Place the peach slices and the rice pudding into a separate mixing bowl then blend until smooth.
3. Gently fold in the yogurt and sugar mix.
4. Now pour the mix into a tub and place in the middle section of the freezer for 5 hours.
5. Once it is ready, serve with the chocolate shavings or the crushed ginger biscuits.
6. This is a great recipe to create with children. Get them involved. They will have fun.

Shortbread Biscuits

Makes 12 biscuits

Ingredients:
- 125g butter
- 55g caster sugar, plus extra to finish (see method)
- 180g plain flour

Method:
1. Preheat the oven to 190c / fan 170c gas 5.
2. Beat the butter and the sugar together until smooth.
3. Stir in the flour to get a smooth paste. Turn on to a work surface and gently roll out until the paste is 1cm/½in thick.
4. Cut into rounds or fingers and place onto a baking tray. Sprinkle with caster sugar and chill in the fridge for 20 minutes.
5. Bake in the oven for 15-20 minutes, or until pale golden-brown. Set aside to cool on a wire rack.

Food for thought

Is canned fruit a good snack?

Canned fruit is a great non-perishable snack. Be sure, though, to choose fruit that is canned in its own juice. All fruit canned in its own juice counts towards your 5-A-DAY. Dried fruits are good for snacking and are a good replacement for fresh fruit. They provide necessary fibre, potassium, and a good amount of nutrients.

Did you know?

Canned fruit provides a great deal of vitamins, nutrients, and natural sugars that fuel and benefit our bodies.

'Recipe tips'

If you open a can of any food, but do not eat it all, make sure you transfer the remaining food into a bowl or other container, cover it then put it in the fridge.

Why?
Because when a can has been opened and the food exposed to the air, the tin or iron from the can might transfer more quickly to the can's contents.

Canned fruits and vegetables can be eaten straight out of the can and provide essential nutrients that you would normally get from fresh fruits and vegetables. Peaches are a surprising source of vitamin C. One study found that the canned kind contain up to four times more vitamin C than fresh peaches.

Apples are low in calories yet high in fibre and water, making them very filling and a great weight loss food!

LITTLE EXTRAS

Bread Rolls made from a Bread Mix

MAKES 4-6

Ingredients:
There is a wide variety of bread mixes now available from plain white to sun-dried tomato and cheddar – all at a very reasonable price!

Method:
1. Pre-heat the oven to 230°C or 210°C for fan assisted ovens or Gas Mark 8.
2. Place bread mix in a bowl and add lukewarm water. Mix for 5 minutes to form a dough. Leave to rest for 5 minutes.
3. Knead the mix and transfer the dough on to a floured surface. Leave it to rest for 5 minutes.
4. Shape the dough into 8-10 individual balls and place on to a greased baking tray. Cover with a damp cloth or loose cling film and leave to rise for 30 minutes or until they double in size.
5. Uncover and bake in the oven for about 15 minutes, until golden brown. When they are ready, they should sound hollow when you tap the base. Turn out and cool on a wire rack.

Why use a bread mix?

- Can save time, especially for us today delivering a cooking session with limited cooking times.
- Easy to follow instructions.
- Good to keep in your store cupboard for emergencies.
- If you have children, it is a great way of getting them interested in baking.
- Can save you money as it avoids having to buy ingredients separately.
- There are so many varieties of bread to choose from, so it is a good way to try out new and different bread types.

Healthy Tomato Ketchup

MAKES 1

Ingredients:
- 125 ml Passata
- 6 tbsp tomato puree
- 60ml water
- 60ml apple cider vinegar or white wine vinegar
- 2 tbsp honey
- ½ tsp garlic powder, seasoning.

Method:
1. Put all the ingredients in a pan and mix well.
2. Simmer over a medium heat for 15 minutes.

You can make this ketchup vegan by swapping the honey for maple syrup. You could also not sweeten it at all, but a little sweetness goes a long way in this recipe.

This recipe will keep in a sterilized bottle in the fridge for a couple of weeks.

Garlic Bread

Homemade Garlic Bread is twice as nice for half the price of buying it!

Ingredients:
- 1 French stick or similar
- 100g butter, room temperature
- 2 tbsp olive oil
- 3 cloves garlic, minced (or very finely chopped)
- 1/4 cup fresh parsley, chopped
- A pinch of salt

Method:
1. Preheat the oven to 200c / fan 180c gas 6. In a bowl, stir together the room temperature butter, olive oil, minced garlic, chopped parsley, and a pinch of salt until relatively smooth.
2. Cut the French bread into two long pieces, then open lengthwise and lay the bread on a baking sheet cut sides facing up. Spread the garlic butter mixture evenly over the open surfaces of the bread.*
3. Bake the bread for 10-15 minutes, or until the edges are golden brown and crispy. Cut the bread into 2-inch sections and serve hot.

Home-made Baked Beans

Ingredients:
- 1 tbsp olive oil
- 1 onion, peeled and diced small
- 2 garlic cloves, finely chopped
- 1 tbsp white or red wine vinegar
- 1 heaped tbsp soft brown sugar
- 400g tin pinto beans, drained and rinsed (or a tin of mixed beans, drained and rinsed)
- 400ml tub passata
- 1 tbsp Dijon mustard (optional)
- 1 tsp smoked paprika
- 1 tbsp Worcestershire sauce (optional)
- Small bunch coriander, chopped (optional)

Method:
- Heat the oil in a small pan.
- Fry onion until starting to brown, then add garlic and cook for 1 min.
- Add vinegar and sugar and cook until onions are caramelised.
- Stir in beans, passata, Worcestershire sauce, Dijon mustard, smoked paprika, and seasoning.
- Simmer for 10-15 mins until thickened.
- Stir in coriander.

Recipe Tips...

If you are short of time and just want to liven up a can of baked beans, add a good splash of Worcestershire sauce and a tbsp of Dijon mustard – this works wonders!

Why did the strawberry cry??

Because it was in a jam!

What is small, round, and giggles a lot?

A tickled onion!

Homemade Jacket Wedges or Chips

Makes 1 Litre

Ingredients:
- 4-5 medium potatoes, washed well – no need to peel
- 4 tbsp vegetable oil
- Good pinch of sea salt and black pepper

Method:
1. Preheat oven 200c / fan 180c gas 6.
2. Cut the potatoes into chunky wedges and pat dry with kitchen roll.
3. Put potatoes, seasoning and oil in a plastic bag or lidded container and shake well.
4. Tip onto a baking tray, making sure they are spread out and not over lapping. Bake in the oven for 35 – 40 minutes or until they are crisp and golden, turning them over halfway through cooking.
5. Serve and enjoy!

Spice your wedges up by adding a tsp of smoked paprika or garlic granules and mixed herbs.

You really cannot beat homemade cooked wedges.

They can be served with absolutely anything – Burgers, chicken, Chilli, Curry -the list is endless!

Basic White Sauce

Ingredients:
- 40g butter
- 40g plain flour
- 500ml milk
- 2 tsp Dijon mustard
- Seasoning

Method:
1. Melt the butter in a saucepan.
2. Stir in the flour and cook for 1-2 minutes.
3. Take the pan off the heat and gradually stir in one-third of the milk. Return to the heat and simmer, stirring, until all the milk is absorbed.
4. Repeat this process, stirring all the time, allowing the sauce to become thick and shiny before adding more milk.
5. When all the milk is added bring to the boil. Simmer gently for 8-10 minutes. Then add the mustard and season with salt and pepper.

This is great for cauliflower cheese – part cook the cauliflower and drain well and place in a baking dish. Add some cheese to the sauce and pour over the cauliflower. Sprinkle the top with a little more grated cheese and bake in the oven 180c/gas 4 for 20-30 minutes until nice and golden.

How did the banana wear her hair?

In bunches!

Why did the tomato go out with the prune?

Because he couldn't find a date!

Food for thought

Why use herbs and spices?

Enjoy simple foods – indulge in the benefits of herbs and spices and let them transform your foods. Herbs and spices have the powers to enhance dishes changing them into something truly brilliant.

- Herbs and spices are a great way to add flavour, colour, and fragrance to dishes without adding extra fat, sugar or salt.
- They have a range of health benefits
- Most herbs, such as parsley, sage, rosemary, mint, basil and thyme, can be used fresh or dried.

What is the difference between herbs and spices?

Spices are seeds and tend to be stronger in flavour than herbs because they are made from the crushed parts of plants that are rich in essential oils. Spices generally come from the roots, stalks, bark, and seeds as well as the flowers and leaves. Herbs are leaves and can be found either fresh or dried, chopped, or whole.

Why are herbs and spices important for your diet?

Both are used to flavour food. Research also shows that they're full of healthy compounds and may therefore have health benefits. Herbs and spices fight inflammation and reduce damage to your body's cells.

"The easiest way to start eating healthier is by preparing your own meals with fresh products"

Did you know?

Avocado's are poisonous to birds

SLOW COOKER

Making the most of a slow cooker!

A slow cooker does not cook anything that couldn't be cooked by any other method. However, the slow cooker does have many benefits.

Why use a slow cooker?
- They are inexpensive to buy
- They are economical to run
- They are perfect for cooking cheaper cuts of meat
- They can save you lots of time when you are busy
- They are good for your health and weight

What are the benefits of a slow cooker?
- Slow cookers rely on long, moisture-rich cooking. You therefore use less oil than you would for conventional cooking thus reducing calorie intake!
- Saves you time if planned properly. Your dinner can be ready for when you get home. So, no more snacking while you are preparing dinner!
- Cook up a batch of slow cooker veggie soup and divide into smaller portions and freeze it so you always have a low-calorie meal on hand!
- Slow cooking requires the minimum of effort. Once you have all your ingredients ready, just throw everything in and your meal cooks itself.

General time guide for adapting recipes

Conventional Recipe	LOW	HIGH
15 – 30 mins	4 – 6 hours	1 ½ - 2 hours
35 – 45 mins	6 – 10 hours	3 – 4 hours
50 mins – 3 hours	8 – 12 hours	4 – 6 hours

Slow cookers are best suited to soups, stews, and dishes like spaghetti Bolognese and Chilli-con-carne.

Should you brown your meat first?

Slow cookers are renowned for being able to cook all the ingredients together at once – and you will get a perfectly good meal as a result. However, while this step is not essential, try to find the time to brown your meat and vegetables in a frying pan beforehand. This will raise your finished dish from the mere 'ok' to a definite "awesome"! The pre-browning helps to intensify the flavours in whatever dish you are making (some slow cookers have an inner pan that you can use directly on your hob for pre-cooking – this also saves on washing up!)

Tips to get more flavour out of your slow cooker recipes:
- Adapt your favourite recipes for cooking in a slow cooker. Reduce the liquid content by a 1/3 rd. as the liquid will not reduce the same as when using a conventional method.
- Don't be tempted to keep taking off the lid as this can add extra time to your cooking. There are exceptions to this such as when the recipe asks you to add more ingredients towards the end of your cooking.
- Rely mostly on the low setting rather than the high one.
- Avoid using frozen ingredients. If you do choose to use such things as frozen peas, for example, add them towards the end and increase the setting to high to cook exceptionally fast.
- Herbs and spices tend to dissipate if cooked for a long time, leaving your dish bland. It is best to add them near the end of cooking.
- Milk, cream, yoghurt and cheeses will break down over long periods of cooking and should be added only in the last half hour.
- Pasta and rice are best added to recipes towards the end of cooking. Ideally pre-cook slightly before adding – you may need to adjust the liquid slightly.
- DO NOT REHEAT FOODS in a slow cooker.

Slow Cooker Porridge

MAKES 4

Ingredients:
- 250g rolled porridge oats
- 1 pint milk
- 2.5 pints water
- 1 pinch salt
- 1 tsp salted butter

Method:
1. Wipe the inside of the slow cooker with a little butter or oil to prevent the porridge sticking while it cooks.
2. Put the remaining ingredients in the slow cooker, stir well, then cook on low for 8 hours.
3. Serve with raisins and a drizzle of honey, or any other topping of your choice!

Slow Cooker Full English Breakfast

MAKES 4

Ingredients:
- 8 sausages
- 8 rashers of bacon
- 4 eggs
- 400g can baked beans
- 400g tinned tomatoes
- 2 knobs of butter
- 1 tbsp milk
- 100g chopped mushrooms
- Seasoning
- 4 slices bread

Method:
1. Grease the inside of the pot with butter.
2. Crack the eggs into a mug, add a splash of milk, knob of butter, salt and pepper to season and mix well. Place the mug into the middle of the slow cooker.
3. Empty the can of baked beans into a mug and place into the middle of the slow cooker in the mug.
4. Empty the can of tomatoes into a mug, season well and place into the middle of the slow cooker in the mug.
5. Put the chopped mushrooms into a mug, add a knob of butter, season with salt and pepper and place into the middle of the slow cooker.
6. Roll the bacon rashers up and place them around the outside of the of the slow cooker.
7. Place the sausages around the outside of the slow cooker.
8. Prepare everything in the slow cooker and just before you go to bed switch on the slow cooker so it will be ready when you wake up! Cook on low for 8 hours.
9. Serve with slices of fresh toast.

What's the most relaxing pasta?

Spa-ghetti

Why do ghosts love health food?

Because it's super-natural!!

Slow Cooker Bolognese

Ingredients:
- 3 tbsp olive oil
- 30g butter
- 1 onion, finely chopped
- 1 celery stalk, finely chopped
- 1 carrot, finely chopped
- 150g pancetta, cubed (or bacon, diced)
- 400g beef mince
- 200ml red wine (optional)
- 1½ tbsp tomato purée
- 200ml beef stock
- 100ml whole milk
- 400g pasta, cooked according to packet instructions
- A little grated cheese, to sprinkle on the top
- Seasoning

Method:
1. Heat the oil and butter in a large saucepan. Add the onion, celery, carrot, and pancetta/bacon and cook on a gentle heat for 10 minutes, or until the onion has softened. Add the mince and brown all over. Increase the heat, add the wine (if using) and cook until evaporated. Dilute the tomato purée in the stock and stir into the meat. Bring to the boil and season.
2. Transfer the mixture to a medium slow-cooker pot. Cover and cook on a low setting for approx. 8 hours. Stir in the milk and cook for 10 minutes before serving. For a large slow-cooker pot, you can make double the quantity, but cooking times remain the same.
3. If the Bolognese is too thin, take off the lid and put on high for 30 minutes and it will thicken up, adjust seasoning if required.
4. Serve the Bolognese with freshly cooked pasta of your choice, sprinkled with cheese.

You can double this up if your slow cooker is big enough and any spare freeze for another day or change it to a cottage pie or chilli!

Veggie Slow Cooker Curry

Ingredients:
- 1 tbsp sunflower oil
- 1 onion, thinly sliced
- 2 garlic cloves, very thinly sliced
- 3 tbsp Indian medium curry paste
- 2 tbsp plain flour
- 500g butternut squash, peeled and cut into roughly into small chunks
- 1 carrot, peeled, halved lengthways, and cut small chunks
- 400g can chopped tomatoes
- 400g can chickpeas, drained and rinsed
- 200g frozen spinach
- 1 tsp soft light brown sugar
- 400ml hot vegetable stock (made with 1 stock cube)
- Freshly cooked rice
- Seasoning

Method:
1. Heat the oil in a large frying pan and gently fry the onion for 5 minutes, or until lightly browned, stirring frequently. Add the garlic and curry paste and cook for 30 seconds more, stirring constantly.
2. Transfer to the slow cooker and add the butternut squash and carrot. Sprinkle over the flour and toss together. Add the tomatoes, chickpeas, frozen spinach, sugar, stock and season.
3. Stir well, cover with the lid and cook on low for 7-8 hours, or until the vegetables are tender and the spices have mellowed. Stir well before serving and adjust seasoning if required.

If you wanted a chicken curry you can add the chicken whilst frying the onions and then carry on adding the other ingredients. You can change the vegetable stock to chicken if preferred!

Slow Cooker Pizza

MAKES 2

Ingredients:
- 1 packet pizza dough (enough for one 12" pizza)
- 350ml passata
- 100g mozzarella grated or torn
- Fresh basil chopped

Method:
1. Oil the inside of the slow cooker - this will help to stop the pizza sticking once during cooking.
2. Roll out the pizza dough to the approximate size of your slow cooker. Place it in and push up the sides of the bowl to form a crust. Poke a few small holes in the centre of the dough to prevent it from bubbling whilst cooking.
3. Top the dough with passata, then sprinkle plenty of grated mozzarella over the top. Add toppings of your choice.
4. Place a piece of kitchen roll under the lid to stop condensation dripping onto your pizza, then cover and cook on low for four hours, or two on high. You'll know it's cooked when the crust starts to brown, and the cheese is bubbling.
5. Allow it to cool slightly, then use a spatula to remove it from the slow cooker. Slice and garnish with chopped basil.

Slow Cooker Whole Chicken

MAKES 4

Ingredients:
- 30g salted butter
- 2 garlic cloves, 1 crushed, 1 whole
- 1 tsp dried oregano
- 1.8kg (approx.) chicken, untied
- 1 large onion, halved and thickly sliced
- 200ml (1/3 pint) chicken or vegetable stock
- Seasoning

Method:
1. Combine the butter with the crushed garlic, oregano and a seasoning of salt and pepper.
2. Starting at the cavity end, gently ease the skin away from the chicken across the breast and spread the butter under the skin, pressing down on the skin to spread it out. Rub the top of the chicken skin with some salt and pepper. Lightly press the whole garlic to crush it and put it in the cavity of the bird.
3. Spread the onion out in the base of the slow cooker.
4. Sit the chicken on top of the onions, breast-side up. Pour the stock in and cover with the slow cooker lid, cook it on high for 4 – 4 1/2 hours or until the chicken is tender and thoroughly cooked.
5. Strain the juices and thicken with some gravy granules.

This can be prepared in the morning and left to cook all day on a lower setting. It will be ready for dinner and needs nothing more than some mashed or baked potatoes and a side of green vegetables.

Food for thought

Why use vegetables in your diet?

Eating a high diet of fresh fruit and vegetables can improve your health and help you to avoid many common diseases. They are rich in vitamins and minerals that can make you feel healthy. They are a good source of dietary fibre and help to raise energy levels.

'Recipe tips'

- Fresh, frozen, or canned vegetables are all healthy choices and will ensure you are getting the right amount of goodness into your diet, whichever one you choose to use.
- Don't skimp on eating vegetables because you're busy and don't have time to prepare them fresh. Instead, use frozen or canned vegetables – they're healthier than you think and even more convenient than fresh.
- The longer you store fresh fruits and vegetables, the more the nutrients decrease – eat within a few days to avoid nutrient loss.

A ham sandwich walks into a bar and orders a beer, bartender says "sorry we don't serve food here"

What do you say to a loud vegetable?

Turnip down!

What is a skeletons favourite food?

Spare Ribs!

What do you get when you cross a dog with a vegetable?

A Broc-Collie

BATCHCOOKING

Batch Cooking

A base recipe is one that can be cooked in bulk and then you can add additional ingredients to make various meals – e.g., mince in a tomato sauce, chicken in a white sauce (see base recipes). The base mince recipe can be used to make meals such as lasagne, Bolognese, chilli-con-carne or cottage pie. The base chicken recipe can be used to make meals such as chicken and pasta bake, creamy chicken and vegetable soup, chicken and broccoli potato topped pie, chicken curry – the list is endless.

Suggestions for use –

Top with buttery mash for a cottage pie

Mix with some cooked pasta and top with grated cheese and bake in the oven to finish off for a pasta bake

Add some kidney beans and chilli powder, serve with rice and tortilla chips

Add herbs and spices with tomato puree to make a curry

Did you Know

When making your favourite recipes, double up on quantity and batch cook – storing meals for later days either in your fridge or freezer.

Batch cooking means you only cook once and you will have additional meals for your freezer when you fancy a night away from the kitchen!

Batch cooking isn't just about the freezer. You can make breakfasts and lunches in advance and have them ready in the fridge!

Meals batch cooked and then divided into smaller portions for your freezer will keep frozen for up to 3 months.

Base Recipe for Mince

Makes 2-3 batches which will serve 4 portions or 8-10 individual portions

Ingredients:
2 med onions. 3-4 carrots, 3-4 celery stalks chopped small
4 cloves garlic, crushed or finely chopped
2 x 400g chopped tinned tomatoes
1kg mince
2-3 tbsps. tomato puree, 500g passata
150ml beef stock
Pinch sugar, 1-2tsp oregano
3 tbsp olive oil, mixed herbs, seasoning

Method:
1. Heat a drop of oil in a large pan and add the garlic, onions, carrots, and celery and cook for 10 minutes or until softened, stirring regularly.
2. Fry the mince in another pan, breaking it up with the back of a wooden spoon. When browned transfer to the veg mix and add the tomato puree, tomatoes, passata, sugar and mix well.
3. Add the beef stock, mixed herbs and seasoning and bring to the boil. Cover and leave to simmer on a low heat for 2 hours or until thickened and reduced.
4. Serve straight away, or leave to cool, batch up and freeze for another day.

Base Recipe for Chicken in a White Sauce

Makes 2-3 batches which will serve 4 portions or 8-10 individual portions

Ingredients:
- 750ml milk
- 3 tbsp olive oil
- 2 chicken stock cubes
- 14 boneless chicken thigh fillets cut into cubes
- 60g plain flour
- 1 onion, finely chopped
- 3 garlic cloves finely chopped
- 1 red and 1 green pepper finely chopped
- Seasoning

Method:
1. Heat the oil in a frying pan and fry the chicken until lightly coloured and then transfer to a plate.
2. Add the onion to the pan and fry for 5 minutes. Then add the garlic and peppers.
3. Add the chicken to the pan along with its juices.
4. Heat the milk and add the stock cubes to it, mix thoroughly.
5. Sprinkle the flour into the pan of chicken and mix. Then add the milk and stock — mix quickly together to avoid any lumps.
6. Add the seasoning to suit your own taste and cook for another 15 – 20 minutes until the chicken is cooked through.

Recipe Tips...

You can make your stock with water instead of milk

You can add other ingredients depending on your taste - chopped carrots, celery, bacon, canned or fresh tomatoes and mushrooms.

You can add additional herbs and spices or flavour with mustard

You can add fresh or frozen vegetables

"Barbara has a great passion for helping people from all walks of life to develop their cooking skills and enjoy healthy food. This book combines Barbara's enthusiasm for cooking with a range of practical recipes and some great advice for cooking on a budget. It's a really useful book to guide and inspire anyone starting off a healthy food journey, cooking with limited ingredients and without any expensive equipment."

David Titman (RNutr)
Experienced food industry professional and registered nutritionist.
Food and nutrition specialist. (RNutr)
RaisingNutrition - CNELM (Centre for Nutrition, Education and Lifestyle Management) High Wycombe, England, UK.

"Having read this publication as someone who is no great shakes at cookery, I ended up much wiser and feeling a lot more confident about putting all the ideas into practice. What a gem of a book! Packed full of sound, practical advice expressed in a clear, easy to understand language. We are given tips about what kind of inexpensive food to use and how to prepare it. On top of all that there is guidance on how to achieve good kitchen management and how to avoid waste. There are menus galore which will help you create nourishing meals (1, 2 or 3 course) using all types of ingredients - fresh, tinned or from a packet, and all reasonably priced if your budget is low. I'm sure there are many of you out there in the community just like me with little experience, theoretical or practical, of creating meals from scratch. For you, this book is a must. Follow the advice given, choose your ingredients carefully and you will certainly find many menus to suit your taste and pocket. What is more, you should never find the prospect of cooking a wholesome meal daunting ever again. I thoroughly recommend this publication to you. Good luck and Happy Cooking!"

Rex Berryman
MFL (modern language teacher) with a degree in French and Spanish. Rex was Head of Department at Hartford school Cheshire working as exams officer and i/c college liaison, and now enjoying retirement as a marker of GCSE's in Spanish.

ACKNOWLEDGEMENTS

I would like to thank the following people for their contribution into creating this book

Thank you to all my friends, family and collegues who have supported me through the past few months, your faith in me has been overwhelming and very much appreciated!!

Thank you also to Andrew Collier for my portrait shots - www.justheadshots.photo.

Thank you to David Titman (RNutr) for all your help and guidance throughout the book with your advice, and for sharing your expert knowledge on nutrition. David is an experienced food industry professional and registered nutritionist. (RNutr).

A huge thank you to Rex Berryman for his time and patience for going through each and every page - correcting my mistakes, of which there were many! Rex is a MFL (modern language teacher) with a degree in French and Spanish. Rex was Head of department at Hartford school Cheshire working as exams officer and i/c college liaison, and now enjoying retirement as a marker of GCSE's in Spanish.

My biggest thanks goes to Ian Downes at Noise Design (www.noisedesign.co.uk) who has pulled together this book and provided the excellent art and design work throughout. His patience in adapting my work and creating the brilliant results is just amazing.

We have worked together on this over the past few months and I cannot thank him enough for his patience, support and professionalism.

Thanks to all the people I have met at cooking sessions, networking, food banks and in the community, for giving me the belief that this is something people want.

Barbara